TEN PRAYERS GOD
ALWAYS SAYS YES TO

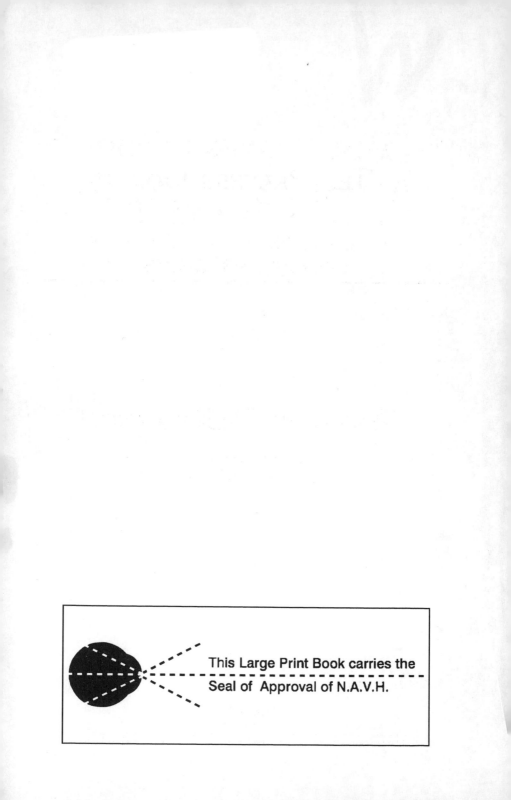

This Large Print Book carries the
Seal of Approval of N.A.V.H.

TEN PRAYERS GOD
ALWAYS SAYS YES TO

DIVINE ANSWERS TO LIFE'S MOST
DIFFICULT PROBLEMS

ANTHONY DESTEFANO

WALKER LARGE PRINT
A part of Gale, Cengage Learning

GALE
CENGAGE Learning

Detroit • New York • San Francisco • New Haven, Conn • Waterville, Maine • London

GALE
CENGAGE Learning˜

LIBRARY OF CONGRESS CATALOGING-IN-PUBLICATION DATA

DeStefano, Anthony.
   Ten prayers God always says yes to : divine answers to life's
most difficult problems / by Anthony DeStefano. — Large print
ed.
      p. cm. — (Walker Large Print originals)
   Includes bibliographical references.
   ISBN-13: 978-1-59415-218-4 (hardcover : alk. paper)
   ISBN-10: 1-59415-218-7 (hardcover : alk. paper)
   1. Prayer — Christianity. 2. Large type books. I. Title. II. Title:
10 prayers God always says yes to.
   BV220.D47 2007b
   248.3'2—dc22   2007042530

Published in 2008 by arrangement with Doubleday, a division of
Random House, Inc.

Printed in the United States of America
1 2 3 4 5 6 7 12 11 10 09 08

This book is for my brothers,
Vito, Carmine, and Salvatore,
and my sister, Elisa

CONTENTS

More things are wrought by prayer than this world dreams of . . .

— Alfred, Lord Tennyson

When we pray properly, sorrows disappear like snow before the sun . . .

— John Vianney, Curé of Ars

INTRODUCTION:

TOO GOOD TO BE TRUE?

This is a book about prayers God always says yes to. Not prayers he says maybe to, not now to, or no to. Not prayers he says yes to sometimes, most times, or once in a while. This book is about prayers God says yes to *all the time.* Are there such prayers? You bet there are!

I know how hard it is for so many in our jaded, cynical culture to approach a book like this without rolling their eyes. But I assure you, this is not a joke or a gimmick. Nor is it one of those self-help books that preach all about personal development, the power of positive thinking, or the ability to "buy real estate with no money down." This is about a spiritual treasure chest that is available to everyone — a treasure chest that few people ever open. This is about prayers that *work* — really, truly work.

Why don't people take advantage of prayers that work? One big reason is that they are so caught up in prayers that *don't* always work. All over the world right now, people are shaking their heads in frustration, asking the question: Why doesn't God answer me when I cry out to him?

Why didn't God cure my mother's cancer? Why doesn't he rescue me from this horrible job? Why doesn't he get me a raise at my job so I can pay my bills? Why didn't he save my wife's brother from that massive heart attack? Why doesn't he send me a husband, or even a boyfriend, so I don't have to be alone anymore? Why did he make my son autistic, when I prayed so hard for healthy children?

Why, why, why?

It's so hard to understand: A supposedly all-powerful, all-knowing, all-loving God — a God who made the sun, the moon, and the stars and has the ability to do absolutely anything he wants — yet so many times he seems to ignore our prayers or, even worse, turns us down flat. Isn't there any explanation that can help keep us from getting angry at him?

There have been thousands of books written about prayer, and millions of sermons preached about it; yet the subject still remains very much a mystery. God's will is inscrutable, the Bible says,[1] and to a certain extent we have to accept that. Yet we *want* to be able to make more sense of it. In the face of all our problems, we want to know why God is often so silent. Are we really alone in the universe, as some claim? And if God *does* exist and *is* listening, why does he say no to us so often? How can we reconcile the idea of a God who says things like "Ask and it shall be given to you; seek and you shall find; knock and it shall be opened unto you"[2] with the undeniable fact that this same God often refuses to grant us what we desire most?

Unfortunately, the answer is something we don't want to hear. God does say no to us an awful lot. Sometimes he says no to us when we come to him with the simplest request. Sometimes he says no to us when we are at our most vulnerable — when we have no one else in the whole world to turn to. Sometimes he says no to us when we get on our knees and desperately plead with him to help us.

Part of the reason for all these "refusals" is that we are looking at prayer in a distorted way. We're viewing it, essentially, with the same kind of consumer mentality with which we view the rest of domestic living: we want *this, that,* and *the other thing,* and we want it *now.*

But God is not some supermarket clerk, and the world is not some huge Wal-Mart. As long as we continue to labor under this misconception, we will continue to get upset every time God says no to us. The harsh reality is that God has some very strict guidelines he goes by when "considering" our prayer requests, and they are sometimes difficult for us to accept.

To start with, there are requests God *always* says no to, no matter how earnestly we pray. For example, if we ask God for something that is obviously bad for our spiritual welfare, he is going to refuse us — period. If a person wants to lie to his friend, or embezzle money from his job, or commit adultery with a coworker, God is not going to give him any assistance. That doesn't mean the person who wants to pursue these things won't be successful anyway. He probably will be. God hardly ever stops us from making the wrong decision — especially when we are in a rebellious state of mind. He has given us the awesome gift of free choice,[3] and that includes the choice to do all kinds of terrible things. But the point remains, while God may allow people to commit crimes, break the commandments, harm their neighbors, and so forth, he certainly isn't standing by providing any divine assistance. A person may make all his lascivious schemes come true, but he will do so on his own — not because of any answered prayers from the Almighty.

Then there are the prayers God says no to for reasons that are not so obvious, even though we may try hard to understand them. There is an old expression that says "God gives us what we *need,* not what we *want.*" What this means is that when God decides to grant a prayer request, he uses a completely different set of criteria than we do. Like a good father, he is not concerned about gratifying our every wish. Instead, he is concerned about only one thing: our *ultimate* good, which boils down to *whether or not we make it to heaven.* Every request we make of God is "evaluated" by him in light of that long-term goal. When we ask God to grant us something, he says yes or no based on what he knows will happen to us in the future as a result of that decision. What direction, spiritually, are we going to go in if he says yes? What will it mean for our soul, over the long haul, if he says no? Will we be more likely to be saved, or damned, as a result of getting what we asked for — or not getting it? Moreover, what will happen to the people around us — those who are affected by what we do and how we act?

Will *they* be more likely to go to heaven or not?

Because of these kinds of global considerations, God sometimes allows things to happen to us that seem terrible, knowing that he will "ultimately" bring good out of them.[4] In these instances, we say that God denies our pleas for help because they are "not in accordance" with his will.[5]

Everyone who has prayed for any length of time has experienced the feeling of letdown that comes with God's refusals. I remember praying very hard once to obtain a certain job in the government. At the time I was in my twenties and not very religious. This particular job was a great opportunity for me to enter the world of politics, and I had all kinds of dreams of running for office one day and making my mark in the world. Because the position was so important to my future, I spent several days and nights intently begging for God's assistance. I made all the usual promises to become a better person, give up my sinful ways, and go to church more often — if only God would grant me *this one little favor.*

As you might guess, I didn't get the job, and as a result, the door was closed to a whole range of career possibilities. I was very upset, and while I didn't stop believing in God, I certainly wasn't happy with him. In fact, I wasn't on very good "speaking terms" with him for a number of months. In retrospect, though, I realize that getting that job would have been the *worst* possible thing for me. Knowing myself and my personality, I can see that I was clearly unsuited to political life. Besides, if God had granted my prayer I would have had to move far away from home. I would have ended up traveling in completely different circles over the next few years, and would never have become involved in the life of the church. As a result, neither my first book nor this one would have been written. In short, my entire life would have been different — and *not* for the better.

Maybe you have a similar story. Looking back over the long course of our lives, it's sometimes easy to see why God has denied us certain requests. Other times it's more difficult — if not impossible. These are the hardest no's for us to accept, because we can't see God's why. When we pray to God for something, we don't have the luxury of twenty-twenty hindsight, nor do we have a crystal ball to look into the future. Naturally, we have a difficult time understanding the wisdom of God's actions, or of his lack of action. We have to go on faith alone.

This is something we don't really want to hear. When we desire something with all our heart — like getting out of debt or being cured of an illness — it sounds so empty and hopeless to say that God will give us only what's "best" for us. Most times we don't care what's best for us in the future; we want instant gratification. We want the answers that *we* feel we need — not the ones God deems necessary.

And so we stop praying, or we pray without conviction, or we begin to doubt the very existence of a God who is supposed to be listening to our prayers. So many people use unanswered prayers as a reason for not believing in God.

But do you know what? There's a flip side to all this. A remarkable and wonderful flip side.

If God gives us only what we need and what is good for our spiritual growth, doesn't it follow that there are certain things that he always *wants* to give us? After all, aren't there certain spiritual favors and graces that are always good for us and that we need all the time? And doesn't that mean, furthermore, that there are certain prayers God *always* says yes to — prayers that he grants at all times, and in all circumstances, because they are always "in accordance with his will"?[6]

You see, there are certain fundamental spiritual needs we have regardless of what happens to us in the future. And there are certain things we can ask God to give us that will be of great benefit to our long-term welfare no matter what the present situation — things that *never* conflict with God's will and that he is always happy to give us. Even allowing for questions about the unknown, unseen future and the mystery of free will, there must, therefore, be certain basic prayers God can always be relied upon to answer in the affirmative.

And indeed there are. Plenty of them! All one has to do is look to the Bible, the words of Christ, the writings of Christian theologians over the centuries, and the testimonies of thousands of people *right now* whose prayers are being answered.

God loves to say yes to us. Not only to "small" prayers, but to big, practical, and profound ones as well. It's just that we don't usually think about these prayers because they are not of the "consumer" variety. We don't realize that if we simply made certain basic requests of God, they would be granted automatically. And once granted, our lives would change — possibly overnight. In fact, our lives would be a hundred times more exciting and passion filled than they are now, and a hundred times less stressful and anxiety-ridden.

Don't believe me?

How would you like to have incredible, unshakable faith — the kind that could withstand any crisis and any amount of suffering? How would you like to have as much courage and strength as the bravest war hero? the wisdom to solve all the problems you'll ever face in life? How would you like to have peace — the kind of deep inner tranquility that can carry you safely and smoothly through all of life's problems? to experience the most passionate feelings of love, intimacy, and connectedness — no matter how alone you may feel now? How would you like to know your destiny — a unique destiny God has chosen for you from the beginning of time, a destiny so grand in scope and heroic in proportions that it dwarfs all your dreams — a destiny you can still have no matter what your age, job, or position in life?

All these things can be yours, and all you have to do is ask. If that sounds too good to be true, why not just give it a try? Instead of debating, denying, or dismissing, why not just take me up on this challenge? Read a few of these chapters, and say a few of the prayers. Then just stand back and watch the results.

I guarantee that before you even get to the last page of this book, your life will begin to change before your eyes.

1
I WISH I COULD BELIEVE

GOD, SHOW ME THAT YOU EXIST

Does God exist?

Can there be a simpler yet more important question in all the universe? Can there be one that has been the source of more mental anguish and emotional confusion in the history of mankind?

It's ironic that a question that so many people struggle with is also one that can be answered most easily by God when we put it in the form of a prayer. For when we lift our minds and hearts in humility and say to God: *"Please show me that you exist. . . . Give me some sign that you are really up there somewhere"* he is only too happy to respond — sometimes with a speed that can astound us.

And yet people often spend decades of their life going round in circles trying to debate God's existence. They analyze the problem, research it, turn it over and over in their minds, go back and forth a thousand

23

times, and at the end of the whole process, they're still not sure.

Why do people get caught in the "faith maze" so often? Probably because so many corollary questions flow from that basic question: Are we alone in the universe? Is death the end of the story? Is there a meaning to suffering? Is there a heaven or hell? Is there an ultimate plan for my life? The problem is that none of these issues can be discussed intelligently if the answer to the first question — *"Does God exist?"* — is no. If there is no God, then any talk about Providence and eternity is absurd. The funeral really is the end of the story, and life has no meaning beyond the day to day. As one of my theology professors used to say, it's the "Looney Tunes" philosophy of life, because like the old Warner Brothers cartoons, the only way to accurately describe death is with the phrase "That's all, folks!"

On the other hand, if there is a God, then a world of possibilities opens up to us. With God, not only does every human being live forever, but all the actions we take and decisions we make have a significance that extends far beyond the present moment. In fact, everything that happens to us in our life — down to the tiniest, most insignificant detail — is mysteriously tied to God's

24

"plan."[1]

There isn't much room for compromise here. Either we're alone in the world or we're not. Either we came about by chance or we were created for a reason. Either death is the end or it's the beginning. Either our situation is ultimately hopeless or it's ultimately blissful. There really can't be two more different or diametrically opposed worldviews.

So how can we come to grips with this most profound question? One way is through simple logic. In the long history of philosophy, many arguments have been put forward concerning the existence of God. Some of the greatest geniuses the world has ever known — Aristotle, Plato, Augustine, Aquinas, Spinoza, Pascal, Descartes, and Kant, to name a few — have made the case that there *is* a God, and that he is a real, living being.

Some of these rational "proofs" are very famous. There is the so-called cosmological argument, for instance, which asks the question "Where did everything come from?" There is the teleological argument, which points to the order and design of the universe and asserts that there must be a "designer." There is the ontological argument, which is based on the concepts of perfection and existence. There are arguments from "efficient causality," from "contingency," from "desire," from "degrees of perfection," from "miracles," from "morality and conscience," and from "reliable testimonies." The list goes on and on.

There isn't time to discuss these proofs here, but all of them are based on logic, observation of the physical world and our internal consciousness, and inductive or deductive reasoning. None is based on Scripture. None attempts to prove God's existence by asserting that "the Bible says this or that."

These logical proofs can be extremely helpful, especially to someone who tends to think that it's not "intelligent" to believe in God or that religion somehow goes against science. But the problem is that sometimes people get so wrapped up in logic that they get *tied up* in it as well. They can forget that the solution they are looking for is right in front of their eyes and doesn't require any arguments at all.

In the case of faith, it's easy to overlook the most fundamental point of all, namely, that God is *not* an argument; he is *not* a syllogism; he is *not* even a concept. God is a living being. He has the ability to know things, to desire things, to create things, and to love things. He is fully aware and involved. He is *alive.*

Why is that so important? Because living beings don't have to be "proved." They can be *shown.* If I want to prove to everyone that my uncle Frank exists, I don't have to mathematically demonstrate that fact. I don't have to produce his birth certificate, passport, driver's license, or Social Security card. I can if I wish, but I don't have to. There's a much simpler solution. If I want, I can just pick up the phone, give him a call, and say, "Hi, Uncle Frank, how are you doing today?" And if anyone had the audacity to doubt that my uncle was really a living, breathing person, and not just some figment of my imagination, all I'd have to do is introduce them to him.

It's a similar situation when we discuss God. Yes, we can come up with all kinds of fancy arguments to prove his existence, but we don't have to. It's not a strict requirement. Because God is a living being, we can simply give him a "call." Since he is really, truly alive, he is going to answer us and have a conversation with us — maybe not in the exact same way as Uncle Frank would if we called him on the phone, but close.

Does that seem too easy? I promise it's not. It's just that most people who have questions about God's existence have never even tried to make contact with him. They've never made a sincere effort to suspend their doubts for one second and say: "God, I don't know if you're up there. In fact, I'm having a big problem believing in you. But if you do exist, will you please do something to show me, so that I know for sure?"

Do you know what will happen if you say this kind of prayer? God is going to answer you. He is going to say YES. He is going to show you that he exists. Why? Because God is not some cosmic joker. He is not interested in playing hide-and-seek with us. His goal is not to confound and confuse us for our entire lives. Yes, he wants us to have faith in something we can't see or touch, but he doesn't expect us to do the impossible. He doesn't expect us to believe in something or someone we can't even communicate with.

You see, communication is really the key to understanding the whole mystery of faith. In fact, the history of the world is really the history of God trying to communicate with mankind.[2] By creating the universe and the planets in the first place, God was essentially "breaking the silence." By creating animals and human beings, he was making

28

conversation possible.[3] By formulating covenants with Adam, Noah, Abraham, Moses, and David, he was taking the step of actually speaking to us.[4] By sending great prophets like Elijah and Isaiah to his chosen people, he was deepening his bond with us and "revealing" himself to us even more clearly.[5] God's most direct act of communication was to become a man in the person of Jesus Christ. By actually walking among us in bodily form and speaking to us plainly in our own language, God was doing everything he could to "talk to us." And by sending his Holy Spirit, first to the Apostles on Pentecost Sunday and then to the rest of the world, God continues to communicate with us to this very day.[6]

The fact is that we have a God who *loves* to communicate. And the reason is that communication is the starting point for any relationship. Everyone has heard it said that God wants to be able to have a relationship with us. There is no truer point in all theology. Indeed, the thrust of God's communication with mankind over the course of history has always been *relational* and not *conceptual*. That's why he actually prefers it when we come to have faith in him through prayer, instead of through logical arguments alone. God doesn't just want to satisfy a curiosity we have, he wants to enter into a friendship with us.[7] When we take the initiative by *asking* him a question, instead of *treating him as a question,* we have actually entered into a dialogue already — whether we know it or not. And dialogue — back-and-forth conversation — is the heart and foundation of any relationship.

Now, we couldn't very well have a relationship with God if the communication was all one way. We couldn't hope to make a bit of progress in the spiritual life if God refused to talk back to us when we ask him the simplest question: "Are you there?" That's why God is always going to answer this question when we pray to him.

How, exactly, will he do that?

Before I attempt to answer that, let me first tell you what he is *not* going to do. If you ask God to show you that he exists, he is not going to hit you over the head with a hammer. He is not going to suddenly appear before your eyes in bodily form. He's not going to perform some tremendous miracle for you. Of course, he can if he wants. He has that option. And he has done that at various times in history with various people, but it's very rare. Chances are he's not going to do it in your case.

And believe me, you don't want him to! I

30

know that it's very tempting to ask God to show you he exists by performing some miracle for you. But that's the *last* thing you want him to do. Why? Perhaps you remember the saying "To whom much is given, much will be expected"?[8] That rule applies here. Let me explain.

Having to believe in a God you can't see is one of the "tests" God gives us in this life. And while it's not always the easiest test in the world, it is certainly a test we can all pass. I remember playing a game with my friends when I was a boy in which we had to close our eyes and fall backward into the hands of another boy standing behind us. It was basically a game of trust. You had to believe that your friend was going to catch you. If he didn't — if he wanted to play a nasty, cruel joke on you — he could actually let you fall and hit the ground. The idea, of course, was that your friend would never do something like that to you. But you still had to trust him, because he *could* let you fall if he wanted. You were putting yourself in his hands. It wasn't a big risk you were taking, but it was still a scary feeling to be falling backward with your eyes closed and your arms folded in front of you.

This is similar to the kind of faith test God gives us in life. By being invisible, he is essentially asking us to close our eyes as we fall back. He is asking us to *trust* him. Now, we can pass the test by believing in him; we can fail it by becoming hardened atheists; or, in rare circumstances, we can have the test taken away from us completely. How so?

If God wishes to, he can always perform a great miracle for us or show us some kind of vision. If he were to do that, we would no longer need to believe in something we couldn't see. We'd have demonstrative, "scientific" evidence instead. And that's exactly what some people ask God to do. They want a miracle. They want to hear the voice of God announcing his presence in a silent room. They want to see an angel appear before their eyes. They want a chair or a desk to move by itself across the floor. They don't want to close their eyes as they fall back into God's hands. They don't want to trust God.

But this is where we really have to be careful. Because if God takes away the test of faith from you, he's going to put another test in its place. And you can be sure that this other test won't be easy.

You see, the overwhelming majority of mankind has to go through life having faith in an invisible God.[9] If you, by some incred-

32

ible act of God's mercy, are excused from that obligation, you can be certain that you will be expected to perform some pretty incredible feat later on, including even the possibility of giving your life.

Remember what happened to Moses? He was given the privilege of seeing the finger of God write the Ten Commandments on Mount Sinai. But then he had to lead a life of hardship and sacrifice in the desert for fifty years and was denied access to the Promised Land. Similarly, Jesus's apostles were given the honor of seeing the Lord perform many wondrous miracles before and after his Resurrection — but all of them had to die horrible martyrs' deaths at the hands of the Romans. (All except John, who was not killed but instead tortured by being dipped into a vat of boiling oil.) Saint Paul was struck blind on the road to Damascus and actually heard God's voice speak to him — but after that he had to suffer greatly, was scourged countless times, shipwrecked twice, and finally beheaded in Rome.[10]

The pages of the Bible and the history of God's church on earth are filled with examples just like these. Like it or not, these are the kinds of tests God offers as *substitutions* for the faith test. Is that something you really want to chance?

I'm not implying that miracles are "bad" or that asking God to perform a miracle for you is wrong. Miracles happen every day. When you are confronted with a problem you can't solve, it's only natural to ask God to intervene on your behalf in a supernatural manner. There's nothing wrong with that. What I'm talking about here are those miracles that are so clear, powerful, and indisputable that they essentially render "faith" in God unnecessary and superfluous. If you ask for that kind of miracle and actually receive one, watch out!

On the other hand, if you simply ask God to show you that he exists, without all the lightning and thunder, you can expect to be answered just as clearly but without the requisite heroic sacrifice. How so?

Very simply, God will give you a *sign* of his presence — a real, genuine, bona fide sign. The exact nature of this sign will be up to him, of course. We always have to remember that God is sovereign and can do anything he likes. But you can be sure it will be something out of the ordinary. Something that — to you, at least — will border on the supernatural. It might be something "big" or something small; dramatic or quiet; profound or simple. It might come to you through the conversation of a

34

friend or while you are at a church service. It might even come to you while you're at a baseball game! God speaks to different people in different ways and at different times.

Whatever kind of sign he gives you, one thing is certain — you will recognize it as a sign. Some *thing* is going to happen to you after you say this prayer — something that has never happened to you in your life before. And when that something happens, the thought is going to pop into your head: *That couldn't have been from me.*

That will be the key — the recognition that something outside yourself was respon- sible for causing something that is now directly impacting your life in a way that couldn't possibly have come from you. It may not be a vision. It may not be the voice of an angel. It may not be anything com- monly associated with miracles. But it will be something powerful nonetheless.

Perhaps an obstacle that has been prevent- ing you from achieving an important goal will suddenly be cleared out of the way. Perhaps you'll be able to overcome some addiction that has had you in its grip for years, quickly and easily. Perhaps a different and completely unrelated prayer you have offered to God will be answered. Perhaps you'll experience a moment of profound insight into a problem that has been a source of constant pain to you. Perhaps you'll be able to conquer some personal evil in your life, or achieve a certain virtue that has up to now evaded you. Perhaps you'll have a close call — a brush with danger or a moment when your life was at risk — and somehow escape it without a scratch. Perhaps some age-old quarrel or animosity that has been a source of great pain will unexpectedly disappear.

No matter how God decides to answer this prayer, your reaction is going to be "How in the world did that happen? How could this possibly have come about? It just doesn't make sense. I didn't plan it. I didn't do any work. I didn't make any phone calls. *I* didn't do anything." There will be a growing conviction in your mind and in your heart that there *must have been* some other force at work. And more important, there will be a growing conviction of the presence of this force.

This is a critical point to understand. The wonder that you'll feel when this prayer is answered will not be the same as what you feel when you experience an ordinary, everyday "coincidence." Everyone has experienced coincidences and weird occurrences

36

in their life. This will not be like them. This will be a direct experience of God's grace, and, as such, it will point directly to the one who is behind it — God.

Now, there are two provisos that I should mention here, and they apply pretty much to every prayer we're going to discuss in this book. The first has to do with the concept of "testing" God.

As the Bible clearly states, we are never permitted to "test" God Almighty.[11] He simply will not stand for that. He will ignore us. If, for instance, you pray to God, "Please show me that you exist," and at the same time think to yourself, "And if you don't show me, I will know that you're not there," then I wouldn't put too much stock in God's answering you. In other words, if your "prayer" is an "if-then" statement — "if you do such and such, I will believe, and if you don't, I won't" — then God is probably going to say no to you. The reason is that this is not really a prayer at all. It's a demand. You're essentially telling God to do something — *or else.*

That is not the proper way to ask God for a sign of his existence. The whole point is to try to be sincere, even if you have tremendous doubts about God. This is a very important distinction. The goal here is to suspend your disbelief — if only temporarily — to give God a chance to enter your life. The idea is to open yourself up, honestly and truly, to receive a special grace from God. That is not the same as being ready to close the door in God's face if God doesn't satisfy you immediately. If you do that, you're not being faithful or even respectful to God; rather, you're treating God likes some trained dog you expect will perform tricks for you.

And this, by the way, is where those logical proofs we talked about earlier come in so handy. In and of themselves, they may not be sufficient to give you the kind of rock solid faith you'd prefer, but they are certainly persuasive enough to make a person say, "There seem to be some very good arguments on the pro-God side, and *because of that,* I am willing to take a chance and pray with sincerity rather than cynicism."

The second proviso has to do with the kind of person you are right now. Let's say that currently you are *not* living a very godly life. In fact, let's say you're doing the opposite — you're breaking a majority of the Ten Commandments; you're lying, having an affair with someone at the office, being selfish, gluttonous, and angry most of the time. In short, you're not doing well spiritually. In theological language, you have what is called a "darkened conscience."

Is this prayer still going to work for you?

Yes! But maybe not in the same way and in the same time frame as it would for someone who doesn't have your vices, someone who has been trying all along to be virtuous. Here's why.

Let's say you took two glasses of water, one clean and clear, the other dark and cloudy, and dropped a shiny gold coin into each of them. Through which glass would it be easier to see the coin fall? Obviously, the glass with the clean water. Well, it's the same with people. If God decides to reach down into your life and touch you in a special way in response to a prayer you've said, it's going to be a little more difficult to see his hand if the life you're leading is dark and cloudy, morally speaking. As a result of all your vices and bad habits, it's going to be tougher for you to recognize God and his saving actions — not necessarily because you're a "bad" person, but simply because it's harder to see through murky water.

It would be the same if you were wearing sunglasses in a dark room. Seeing exactly what was going on around you might be a challenge. But just because it might be a challenge doesn't mean it would be impossible. If you are living an immoral sort of existence now, it might take you a little longer to discern the hand of God in your life — but you will discern it. God is going to answer this prayer no matter what level of spirituality you are at. You can be a great sinner or a great saint; either way, if you ask God to show you that he exists, he is going to say yes. Once again, God *wants* to communicate with us. He wants us to believe in him. He wants us to have a relationship with him. This is a matter of Judeo-Christian doctrine. Saint Paul summed it up best when he said: "God wills that all come to a knowledge of the truth." Not just the holy, not just the religious, not just the virtuous — but all.[12]

So don't let the fact that you have failings discourage you from saying this prayer. For the moment, just go forward, full speed ahead. If you do, the other problems and vices you have will start taking care of themselves. As you begin to feel the presence of God in your life, you will also begin to experience an inner freedom and peace that goes hand in hand with grace. You'll find that it will be much easier to clean up the rest of your life. We'll be talking a lot more about this in later chapters, but for now understand that the best thing you can do if you are an atheist, agnostic, or doubting Thomas is simply to open up and ask God to show you that he is there.

The writer C. S. Lewis once said that whatever God takes from you with his left hand, he always gives back with his right — in abundance. God may have taken away our ability to see him with our eyes, but that is only because he has something better in mind for us. Just as a blind man is forced to use his other senses to experience the world, God forces us to see him through different senses — through divine lenses, if you will. In doing so, he gives us not only the ability to see him, but also the ability to actually become part of him. The intimacy that we can share with an invisible God is not simply exterior, but deeply interior as well. If we respond to God in faith, we will eventually come to a point where the relationship we have with him is so close and so intimate that we will be as sure of his existence as we are of our own.

In practical terms, this means that when you say this prayer, your faith will begin to grow — slowly at first, and then geometrically. When God starts to reveal himself to you, that will only be the beginning. "Draw near to him and he will draw near to you," the Bible says.[13] The more steps you take toward God, the closer he will come to you. Like someone lying in the sun at the beach getting darker by the hour, your faith is going to get deeper and deeper the more time you are exposed to the light of God. It may take some time, but believe me, you are going to get to the point where you no longer have *any* doubts about his existence. In fact, you will begin to develop a kind of certainty about God that you have never experienced about *anything* else.

With this new kind of certitude, you will also begin to have what I can only describe as a feeling of invincibility — a feeling that nothing can touch you. You'll walk around feeling as safe as a soldier in a tank, or a policeman wearing a bullet-proof vest. You'll have the sense that if the whole world crumbled around you, you would remain standing, unharmed and unscathed. That's the kind of spiritual armor this prayer will give you.

This tremendous sense of well-being will come directly from the fact that you will know — not hope, not wish, not suspect, but *know* — that there is an almighty power that created the universe, and that he is with you every moment of the day and night. Problems of every kind — problems that formerly caused untold amounts of pain and anxiety — will completely lose their crippling effect on you. Problems with money, with coworkers, problems with family members, illnesses, bouts of loneliness and depression — even death itself — will never hold the same kind of power over your life.

Don't misunderstand what I'm saying. I'm not claiming that these problems will magically disappear. I'm saying that the way you feel about them will change drastically — to the point where you'll be able to deal with every problem in your life from a position of strength. That is one of the graces God generously bestows along with faith.

I'm also not saying that you will never again have doubts about God. You may very well have setbacks along the way — temporary crises of faith that come about because of the death of a loved one or because of some other traumatic event in your life. But these won't last long. I can't emphasize this point enough: believing in God is not some phase you go through. It's not a hobby you lose interest in or a love affair that stops being passionate. True faith is a constant progression. If you were to plot the kind of faith I'm talking about on a graph, you might see some places where there were dips and downturns, but the general movement will always be up. Once you get started on this road, God's objective is always the same. He wants you to have a kind of superfaith — an invincible, heroic, indestructible faith.

And it all starts with one simple prayer: *God, please show me that you exist.*

There is a beautiful nineteenth-century painting that illustrates this point well. It's called *The Light of the World.* In it, Christ is shown holding a lantern, standing outside a little cottage on a dark, stormy night. He is knocking on the door of the home, waiting to be let in, but the occupant, unseen behind the door, does nothing. The figure of Christ, bathed in a golden green light, is supremely serene and looks as if he is prepared to stay outside the cottage door knocking forever. It is a striking image because of what it says about the light of truth in a dark world. But the really interesting thing about the painting is that there is a curious detail missing. If you look closely at the door of the home, you will see that there is not a knob or a latch anywhere to be found. Why? It can't be that the artist forgot to put it in. Rather, he was making a sublime theological point: the door to the human heart can be opened only *from the inside.* God will never force his way in.

In this chapter, we've been talking almost as if *we* were the ones who were responsible for making the first move with God. But really that's not the case. Even though it might at first appear to us as though we are taking the initiative by asking God to show us that he exists, in reality, God is the one who is constantly knocking at the door of our hearts.[14] When we ignore him — even when we go for years and years without ever thinking about him — he still remains outside, waiting, knocking. The fact that we desire to know him, that we desire to search for him, even when we have serious doubts about him, is possible only because he is outside the door, quietly but persistently requesting entrance.

The amazing thing is that we really don't have to do very much to let him in. We don't have to study all the arguments for and against his existence, we don't have to torture ourselves with questions about death and the afterlife, we don't have to ask for a miraculous vision to be given to us, we don't have to consult with any experts, read a lot of difficult books, or take a public opinion poll.

All we have to do is ask one simple question in the form of a prayer. Like the owner of that little cottage in the painting, when we say in the dark of the night: "Who's there . . . is anyone there?" we won't have long to wait for a response. By asking that question, sincerely and humbly, we are essentially opening the door to God. He will not stay outside in the storm. He is going to walk right through the door and into your heart.

And when that happens, I promise nothing in your life will ever be the same.

2
WHY SHOULD I GET INVOLVED?

GOD, MAKE ME AN INSTRUMENT

Do you want to know the prayer God answers fastest? The prayer God says yes to most consistently? The prayer he answers with the most pleasure and least fuss or conditions? It's a very old prayer — as old as Christianity itself — and it can be formulated in many different ways.

At first glance, it may not seem all that exciting. It may not seem to carry with it the promise of any great benefits or blessing. But I'll tell you this: it is one *effective* prayer. In fact, the prayer I'm talking about is so potent that if it were sold in a supermarket, it would have to come with a warning label: "Don't pray this unless you are prepared for instant results!"

What is this prayer that generates such an immediate and surefire response from God? Basically, it's simply a request: "Please, Lord, make me an instrument to carry out some important mission of mercy for you."

In other words, *"Please use me to help someone in need."*

I'm not exaggerating when I say that God says yes to this prayer quickly. In fact, one of the reasons that we're discussing it now, right after a chapter on faith, is that the speed, consistency, and reliability with which God answers this prayer can almost be taken as a *proof* of his existence.

Stay with me here. If you sincerely say to God, "Make me an instrument," you are going to get such an immediate response that you will find it very difficult to have any doubts about the presence of the Almighty. These four little words will escape your lips and within seconds, hours, days, or weeks (certainly not more than weeks), you are going to be answered. And since this is going to happen every single time you pray it, any lingering questions you have about God's existence will soon be dispelled.

Mark my words, after you say this prayer, someone in need is going to practically show up on your doorstep — and he or she is going to be in dire straits. Emotionally, psychologically, physically, financially — you name it — they are going to have some kind of serious problem. The person may be a friend, an enemy, a family member, or a complete stranger. But they're going to be in bad shape. And you are going to be the only person in the world who can help them.

Why does this prayer work so fast? I can think of many reasons. In fact, I know of very few prayers in which so many spiritual laws converge.

To begin with, it's important to understand that God has been using "instruments" since he first created the world. This is nothing new to him. In fact, God's whole plan of salvation has been to save *us* through *us* — through people just like you and me. That's why he doesn't perform miracles every minute of the day but instead lets us take part in the business of life by making things happen ourselves. That's why he doesn't go about creating human beings out of thin air. Instead, he lets us play a pretty enormous role through the process of procreation. That's why down through the centuries, when God has wanted to communicate important messages to us, he hasn't simply shouted out his commands from heaven. Rather, he has used prophets and kings and judges as ministers of his word. And that's why, when God chose to save the world, he did it through his only son — Jesus Christ — who was fully God and fully human. He could have redeemed us in any number of ways, but he wanted us to be saved by one like us.

So when we ask to be used as instruments of the Lord, we are actually employing a "pattern" that God himself uses all the time. We are essentially "modeling" ourselves after God. Of course he's going to want to grant our request.

A second reason he always honors this prayer is that it ties in directly to his great command "Love thy neighbor."

Now, "love" is a very misunderstood word today. Most people treat it as a silly cliché. They look at love as no more than a concoction of warm, gooey feelings. Not only is this a false way of viewing love, it's juvenile as well. It hardly does justice to such an immense and powerful experience. This idea of love might make for a good romantic movie or a catchy pop tune, but it certainly doesn't jibe with real life or with Scripture. The Bible is so obviously filled with death, sacrifice, righteous anger, and suffering that love simply has to mean more than nice, mushy feelings.

And, indeed, there is another way to look at love — the way God looks at it.

Love has only one meaning — self-giving sacrifice. Doing something for someone else — even when we don't want to, even when every fiber of our being tells us not to — is the true definition of love. It's no wonder Christ said that the greatest act of love is to sacrifice your life for a friend.[1] It all comes down to giving yourself away.

Christ himself taught us this most perfectly during his Passion. The night before he died, he said to his apostles, "This is my body, given up for you."[2] He didn't try to preserve his body at all costs. He was willing to sacrifice it for us. A few hours after he said these words, he put them into action, laying down his life so that all of us could have our sins forgiven and enjoy eternal happiness in heaven. That's why the best, truest symbol of love is not the heart, not the wedding ring, not cupid's arrow. It is the Cross.

There's a well-known quote from the Bible that is extremely difficult to interpret unless you understand love from this perspective. In the Gospel of Matthew, Christ tells a group of disciples: "Where two or three come together in my name, *I am there in the midst of them.*"[3] What could he have possibly meant by that? Why would he use the phrase "two or three people" instead of just one? After all, can't God be present to just one person? Can't he be there for just you or me alone? Does there have to be a group of people hanging around for God to "show up"?

The answer is "of course not." God is present even when *nobody* is there. But that's not what Christ was talking about. Christ was making a specific theological point. He was teaching us the true meaning of love. When "two or three" people are present in a particular place and at a particular time, it is possible for one of those people to *give himself away* in love. In other words, it is possible for that person to "love his neighbor." And it is when you love your neighbor that God is most truly and fully present.

Are you beginning to see why this prayer always works? It ties into the very *essence* of God's being, which is love. If we pray for God to use us as an instrument to help someone else, we are really praying to be God-like. We are really praying for God himself to come into our lives and act through us. Why would God contradict his very being by denying us that which he has already asked — in fact commanded — us to do?

We see this truth expressed throughout the pages of Scripture. Whenever someone in the Bible has a powerful experience of God, his or her first impulse is always to go out and help someone else. Take the example of Mary. When the angel Gabriel visited her in Nazareth and gave her the news that God had chosen her to be the mother of his only son, he also informed her that her cousin Elizabeth was going to have a baby — a baby who would grow up to be John the Baptist.[4]

In the history of the world, no one has ever had a more profound encounter with God than Mary did at that moment. The Gospel says that the Holy Spirit literally "overshadowed her" and that Jesus Christ — the second person of the Holy Trinity — was conceived in her womb.

Now, what did Mary do after this experience? Did she go off on a spiritual retreat? Did she lock herself in her room and meditate? Did she attempt to reassess her relationship with God? All these actions would have been perfectly understandable. After all, this was an incredible thing that occurred. No human being had ever been in closer "union" with God. The experience was going to change Mary's life drastically, and she knew it. She would have been more than justified to take a few weeks to mull things over in her mind, to pray intensely and try to come to grips with the mystery of what had happened to her.

But no, she didn't do any of these things. Instead Mary left Nazareth immediately and rushed to the side of her cousin in order to help her. And she stayed at her side for three months, until Elizabeth's baby was born.[5] Reading the Gospel account, it almost seems as if Mary was paying more attention to what the angel had said about Elizabeth than what he had said about her!

And here we have the perfect model of *service* that results from every genuine encounter with God. Whenever we meet God — who is love — we are going to be inspired to do that which love impels us to do, namely, give ourselves away to those in need.

Well, if prayer is anything at all, it is an encounter with God. For us it may not be as intense, intimate, and direct an encounter as Mary experienced, but it is still a form of union with the Almighty. Thus, when we sincerely try to pray, God is going to lead us, inevitably, to helping others. Sooner or later, the act of praying is going to result in the act of loving your neighbor. That goes for every prayer you can think of, not just the ones in this book. The reason that this prayer in particular is so fast acting is because when you say to God, "Make me an instrument," you are *explicitly* asking for something God intends to give you anyway. Therefore not only is he going to say yes to you, but he is going to speed up the process, as well.

But there's even more. This prayer also ties in to one of the greatest mysteries of the world — human suffering.

Suffering is a fact of life — and a terrible one at that. Unfortunately, it comes in a million different shapes and sizes. It can be as annoying as a mosquito bite or as tragic as the death of a child. We first experience suffering when we're babies in the crib, crying because we're hungry and alone. For many of us, our suffering doesn't end until we're old and gray, our bodies spent, alone again — this time in a coffin. Suffering can be searing, draining, agonizing, debilitating, exhausting, and relentless. Saddest of all, it is inevitable.

As believers, we are taught that God didn't intend for human beings to suffer when he first created us; that our first parents, Adam and Eve, did something horribly disobedient and brought all this evil upon us. We're also taught that our suffering won't last forever. That God became a man in the person of Jesus Christ in order to make up for Adam's sin, and that because of his saving action on the Cross, he opened up the gates of heaven to us. Thus, while we still have to go through pain, suffering, and death on earth, we can all look forward to the day when we will rise again, in our bodies, and live forever in paradise with our family and friends.

That's what Christianity teaches. Unfortunately, it's a very *hard* teaching. No matter how true it may be, it doesn't always make us feel any better, especially when we're standing in a dreary funeral home, staring at someone we love lying in a box. Which brings us back, once again, to our prayer.

There is so much suffering in the world — God really has his hands full. It's not that he can't manage the situation by himself. He can. It's just that there's so much more *good* that can be accomplished if we try to become like him. When we offer to assist someone in need, not only are we reducing the amount of aggregate suffering in the world, but we are also helping to make ourselves into the kind of creatures God wants us to be — by loving others as he does. By combining these two actions, what we are ultimately doing is "helping God" pull good out of bad — which is one of the main reasons he allows suffering in the first place. That's why God absolutely loves it when we tell him that we are willing to take on other people's problems. For practical as well as theological reasons, he is only too happy to "share" his enormous burden with us.

The question for us is, how, exactly, will God respond to this prayer when we say it?

And the answer is — a *million* different ways. All you have to do is think about all the people you know who are suffering right now. At this very moment, there are people who are crying because someone they loved died last week. There are people who are terrified because they just received news that their X-rays revealed a "spot" on their liver or lung. There are people who are wringing their hands in frustration because their child is addicted to drugs. There are people who are at their wits' end because they just can't take the pressure of paying their bills anymore. There are people who are sobbing themselves to sleep because they are tired of being alone, with no one to love them the way they need to be loved or deserve to be loved. There are people who are suffering from terrible depression, or from excruciating psychological, emotional, and physical pain.

When you say to God, "Make me an instrument," all God really has to do is channel some of these folks in your direction. There's no need for him to perform any great miracles. No need for him to part the Red Sea. No need for him to send any angels. He simply has to steer them your way. Like a conductor in a railway station who pulls a lever in order to make the tracks switch, God simply pulls a lever in heaven, and a veritable trainload of suffering people will automatically be rerouted in your direction!

Then it's up to you. You'll have to figure out the best way to help them. It may be as simple as offering a kind word of advice or lending them a few dollars; it may be as difficult as donating a kidney or saving their life in a fire. Whatever you have to do, though, you can be sure that you will be able to rise to the occasion. If God sends you someone to assist, he is also going to give you the time, the resources, and the wherewithal to do it. He's not about to answer such a wonderfully selfless prayer and then leave you stranded. Never worry about your lack of ability, your shaky finances, or any other problems you have that might hinder you from carrying out your mission of mercy. No matter what your personal situation, when the moment comes to help someone in need, you will be given all the wisdom and means necessary to be successful. Of that you should have no doubt.

And it doesn't matter how old you are or what physical condition you're in, either. You can be in a hospital bed down to your last few breaths, and God is still going to send you someone whom you can help. It might be the nurse attending you. It might be the patient in the next bed. It might be one of your visitors. You might not even be able to help them with words. It might just be your quiet example they need to see most. Or maybe you'll only be able to say a few prayers for them. Who knows? You can be sure of one thing, though. Whomever God chooses to send to that hospital bed will have the possibility of coming away a better, happier person because of having encountered you.

Naturally, if you're young and healthy, there are no limits to the kind of interesting people God can send your way. In fact, God might not just give you one or two individuals to assist; he might give you a whole cause to get involved in. After all, there are millions of people throughout the world whose rights are being trampled on. Right here in our own country, the dignity of human life is under fierce attack. In answer to this prayer, you might be shown one of these great causes and asked by God to throw yourself headlong into it. He might reveal to you an incredible vocation you didn't even know you had.

Of course you have to be careful. No matter how great the cause, it's essential that you never neglect your other duties in life. There are some folks who get so immersed in worthy causes that they forget the responsibilities they have to their spouse and their children and their job. Fulfilling your God-given obligation to your family always comes first. But, that aside, there is no doubt that saying this prayer will *radically* change your life.

And that leads us to a final question — a question that might sound a bit sacrilegious, but one that might be on the minds of a few readers. Given how effective this prayer is, and the kind of impact it is sure to have on your life, *why would anyone ever say it?*

I mean, why would anyone ask for more problems? Don't we have enough of our own? Why would we ask God to use us as instruments to alleviate the suffering of others, when we have so much in our lives to deal with already? After all, we're not required to be gluttons for punishment. It doesn't seem to make any sense.

And that's the point.

"Whoever tries to save his life will lose it," the Gospel says, "and whoever loses his life will save it."[6] Ultimately, this paradox contains the whole key to our happiness — both here and in the next world. Saying this prayer is actually going to make you a much happier person than you are right now. Happiness is the thing God is going to give you in return for your selflessness.

In fact, the more problems you have, the greater reason there is for you to say this prayer. The kind of confidence and faith it takes to ask for more problems — even other people's — is very appealing to God. You've heard the expression "Fight fire with fire"? That's exactly what this is. It's the kind of bold and aggressive approach to life's challenges that will positively endear you to God.

Some of this is just basic psychology. When we are hurting from something, the best therapy is often to look *outside* ourselves. When all our attention is directed inward — to our own little world — we often get fixated, sometimes to an unhealthy degree. Helping others not only distracts us, it gives us a chance to see that we aren't the only ones out there who are suffering — that our problems aren't quite so bad after all, at least relatively speaking. The sense of perspective we get from helping others is essential to helping us develop a positive outlook on life.

But of course there are also spiritual reasons for helping others. We've already talked about the fact that when we serve our neighbors, we are acting in "union" with God. Well, this union has consequences. C. S. Lewis said that human beings are like cars that are designed and built to run on a special type of "fuel" — God. When we deprive ourselves of that fuel for long periods of time, the same thing that happens to cars happens to us: we start riding rough and, eventually, we break down. It's impossible for us to "run on empty" for very long without experiencing problems in every area of our life. On the other hand, acting in union with God has the opposite effect — we begin to "run" much better, much more smoothly. We become stronger, healthier, and more powerful. Saying this prayer is equivalent to filling ourselves up with a full tank of high-octane gasoline. We're going to start feeling rejuvenated; we're going to start feeling *great.*

In fact, not only are we going to experience true happiness, but we're going to feel a profound sense of fulfillment as well. After you get into the habit of saying this prayer, you'll never again come to the end of a day and think that it was "wasted." As long as you try your best to assist the people God sends to you, you are going to know that you are achieving something immensely important in life. And since God is good, he's not about to keep all that you do a secret. At various times he's going to show you the fruits of your labors. He'll reveal to you the wonderful effect you've had on other people's lives. The satisfaction you ultimately get from this will be far greater than *any* of your other accomplishments in life.

And the benefits don't even stop there. For when we ask God to use us as instruments to solve other people's problems, God begins in earnest to assist us with *our* problems as well. I don't mean to imply that there is some kind of quid pro quo here — "I'll scratch your back, God, if you scratch mine" — I only mean to say that the natural outcome of helping others is that we get to share in the benefits ourselves — sometimes to an even greater degree than the people we're assisting. Don't be surprised if, after saying this prayer, your own affairs begin to straighten themselves out. Don't be surprised if you get some angelic assistance when it comes to dealing with your bills, your marital difficulties, and your problems at work. Don't be surprised if you start running into people who are suddenly interested in helping *you,* the same way you are helping others. In many ways, it's the "what goes around comes around" dynamic in reverse.

You see, if God is going to use you as an instrument, he is going to begin fashioning and shaping you so that you can be the *best possible instrument.* It's true that the Lord often uses flawed, sinful people to accomplish his will. But he doesn't let them remain in that condition for long. That's because a person obviously can't function as an effective instrument if he or she is consumed by all kinds of anxiety problems, money problems, and relationship problems. Therefore if you show a willingness to help God in the monumental task of alleviating suffering, God is going to immediately start "working" on you. Think about it — what's the first thing a writer does before he puts pencil to paper? He sharpens that pencil! Well, God is the author of the universe. He's not about to write for any long stretch of time with a dull, crooked pencil. He's going to begin "sharpening" you.

The result is that your life is going to change for the better — *you* are going to change for the better. Whether you like it or not, you are going to start improving in all sorts of areas. In order to be a channel of God's grace, you are going to necessarily have to grow in grace yourself. You may not specifically set out to obtain all the benefits that come with God's grace, but you are going to get them anyway, almost by default.

What are those things? Well, to start with, peace, wisdom, love, freedom, good judgment, companionship, courage, excitement, and adventure — all the things we're going to be talking about in this book. Asking God to make you an instrument is really the same thing as asking him to give you a shortcut to complete fulfillment.

When you think about it, that's an awful lot to get for one little prayer.

3
WHAT'S IN IT FOR ME?

GOD, OUTDO ME IN GENEROSITY

When I was a little boy, my mother used to say to me, "If you give something you own away to somebody else, God will always give you back *two* things in return."

Well, I've learned a lot about God and spirituality since then: I've studied the great theologians — plowed through Augustine, Aquinas, Luther, Calvin, and Newman; met with some of the most learned religious leaders of our time; visited the sacred places of the Bible; spent hundreds of hours poring over texts, mulling over problems, and thinking through scriptural questions. Do you know what I've discovered? That when it comes to the subject of God and the material blessings he is willing to bestow on us, my mother was as right and as accurate as any theologian who ever lived!

And isn't that always the case when it comes to real spiritual truths? God wants to bless everyone; he wants to have a relationship with everyone; he wants everyone to go to heaven — not just the scholars. So when he speaks to us, he doesn't just use language that only theologians and philosophers can understand. His message and his word are truly universal. That doesn't mean we don't need the guidance of his church. We certainly do — very much so. It's just that we don't always have to have some professor or Scripture expert hovering over our heads deciphering everything that God wants us to do.

We see this most clearly in the sayings of Christ in the Bible. When we read sacred Scripture, we recognize immediately that the simple words of Jesus are able to communicate to a vast range of people. For instance, it's possible to find dozens of scholarly books interpreting the statement: *". . . Seek first the kingdom of God and His righteousness, and all these things will be given to you as well."*[1] But at the same time, it's also possible for the most uneducated, illiterate, unworldly person to correctly understand its meaning, even on first hearing.[2]

I'm sure this can be a little annoying to the theologians! Yet it's absolutely true. Of course, none of this is meant to disparage the study of theology. God's ways are so different from ours and his mind is so unfathomable to our little brains that even his simplest, clearest statements have enough depth behind them to provide a lifetime of study to anyone interested.[3] Certain biblical sayings, too, seem to be so ambiguous and are so obviously prone to misinterpretation that we need to be extremely careful in discerning their meaning. Their basic truth may be self-evident, but they can be very easily misunderstood and misconstrued, especially if taken out of context. And in some unfortunate cases, they might even be purposely distorted by unscrupulous individuals who aren't the least bit concerned about advancing the Gospel, but care only about advancing themselves.

So it is with the prayer we're going to be discussing in the next few pages: *"God, please outdo me in generosity."*

In religious circles, there has always been a great deal of confusion surrounding the subject of material blessings. You might say that there are two equal but opposite errors spiritual people sometimes fall into. One is to view money and wealth as something very bad — even evil. This is the "Gospel of Poverty" mentality, and according to its tenets, anyone who tries to accumulate wealth is essentially following the will of the devil and is on the path to death and destruction. The people who hold this view believe that God doesn't like the "rich" at all and that money is something the Bible condemns outright. They think, therefore, that, with very few exceptions, eating at fancy restaurants or buying expensive jewelry or attending lavish events or wearing nice clothing or indulging in *any* kind of luxury should be frowned upon.

Then there is the opposite view — the "Gospel of Prosperity." This is the theory expounded by some of the "name-it-and-claim-it" preachers you see on television. You know the ones I mean — the ones who sport Rolex watches, Armani ties, flashy cuff links, and even flashier smiles. According to these folks, having a lot of money is an unreservedly wonderful thing and anyone who says otherwise is simply misunderstanding the Bible. Money is just another one of God's many blessings, they claim — and one that God wants to freely bestow on anyone who approaches him. God loves rich people and wants *everyone* to be a millionaire. In fact, all you really have to do to amass abundant wealth is rid yourself of guilt, pray hard to the Lord, and — while you're at it — "send the largest possible donation to this ministry."

Both views miss the mark. They both emphasize various scriptural truths to the exclusion of others and, as a result, fail to tell the whole story. What does the Bible say about the subject of money, and what has Christian theology taught about it for two thousand years?

Well, for one thing, it should be apparent to anyone who even glances at the Bible that God can be very tough on the rich. There isn't enough space here to cite all the scriptural passages that warn of the pitfalls of having money — but there are dozens. Everyone has heard the statement: "It is easier for a camel to go through the eye of a needle than for a rich man to enter the kingdom of heaven."[4] Or "The love of money is a root of all evil."[5] Or "Do not store up treasures for yourself on earth, where moths and rust corrupts and where thieves break in and steal, but rather store up for yourself treasure in heaven."[6]

There are quotes like these spread throughout Scripture. They can be a little frightening to anyone who believes in God and, at the same time, has committed himself to becoming affluent. Yet one of the first things to notice about these biblical warmings is that none of them criticizes money *itself.* None of them says that it is in any way sinful to possess money or to accumulate wealth. What they do say very clearly, however, is that having money can be extremely *dangerous.*

Why is money dangerous? Because money has the power to separate a person from God in a way that few other things in life can. Money can give us a feeling of invincibility. It can make us think that we have everything we need in order to be happy and fulfilled, and that we don't have to rely on anyone — including God. This attitude breeds a kind of spiritual complacency that is extremely dangerous because it is so obviously untrue. No matter how rich we might be, things can change for the worse in the blink of an eye. I remember once being the guest of a friend at a magnificent hotel in Rome. The suite I was given was truly opulent, full of marble and mirrors and ceilings gilded with gold, and a balcony overlooking the Vatican. The only problem was that I caught a flu bug the first day I arrived and spent the next three days in agony. I remember lying facedown on the cold marble floor, my eyes looking up at the beautiful paintings on the wall and the antique vases full of flowers, groaning to myself and thinking, how can this be? I'm in a palace — an actual palace — and I can't enjoy it. Why? Because of a tiny little bug!

And this was just a stomachache. So many people receive death sentences from their physicians every day: terminal cancer, terminal emphysema, terminal heart disease. Indeed, we are all living "under the shadow of the gallows." Have you ever heard the saying "The same God that gave you the morning does not promise you the evening"? Never were truer words written. People who fail to rely on God for help because they happen to be able to afford a housecleaner, a butler, and a personal trainer are truly gambling with their lives — because they are just a doctor's visit away from tragedy. When the bad news comes (and it comes to everybody at some point), they have no one to turn to.

The status money confers on us can also get us into a lot of trouble. Because we live in a upscale neighborhood, drive a fancy car, or take nice vacations, it's only natural for us to think that we are special — that we are, in fact, "superior" to everyone else. People forget that this is the very same kind of spiritual pride that got Satan kicked out of heaven![7] It's particularly insidious because it's so easy to fool ourselves into thinking that we're not really being prideful. We often justify our feelings of superiority by saying that we are simply more "successful" than the next person, or more "intelligent" or more "talented," or that we have more "business savvy."[8] All of these things might be true, but too often what we are really thinking to ourselves is that we are *better* than the next person. This is a very dangerous way of looking at things because, once again, it is patently false. The homeless drug addict we see on the street every day on our way home from work may very well make it to heaven before we do. And he may indeed have a higher, more glorious place in paradise than us.[9] "Better" is a word we always have to be very careful about when applying to ourselves. God may have a completely different opinion on the matter.

Finally, having money gives us the possibility of creating endless diversions for ourselves — diversions poor people just don't have. Some of these diversions are good, like having the ability to choose where to live, where to go on vacation, or which school to send our children to. Some are bad, like having enough money to indulge in any kind of sordid vice we like without getting caught (or convicted). Whether positive or negative, though, these diversions all have the power to fill up our days, leaving precious little time for prayer and worship of God.[10] How many wealthy old men have spent decades of their life amassing pretty toys — be they houses, cars, electronic gadgets, or summer homes — moving from pleasure to pleasure, without the slightest thought about God and what is important to him? Then, when they finally come to the end of their days and realize that life is a lot more than the shiny trinkets they've collected, it's too late. It's not that they can't turn back to God at the last minute — they can — it's just that they've already wasted so much time.

So yes, for all these reasons and many more, money can become an idol to us and replace God in our minds and hearts.[11] Thus it can be extremely dangerous. For a certain percentage of people — especially those addicted to status or prone to pride or easily tempted to vice — being rich is probably the worst thing that could ever happen to them, spiritually speaking.[12]

Yet we mustn't jump the gun and issue a summary judgment against the rich just because of the potential dangers of wealth. Not only would that be unfair to them, but it would be unfair to God, who is the one who created wealth to begin with. Indeed, we don't have to look very far to find a biblical defense of money. In fact, the same pious Christians who often condemn the rich at every turn run into a huge stumbling block right at the center of the Gospel. At the very climax of biblical history, we meet up with a certain rich man who practically turns the Gospel of Poverty on its head.

The rich man's name was Joseph of Arimathea, and he was a disciple of Jesus.[13] Joseph was a prominent and wealthy member of the Sanhedrin who opposed their decision to kill Jesus. After the Crucifixion, Joseph was the only one who had the courage to go to Pontius Pilate and ask for Jesus's body. When he was granted permission, he took Jesus off the cross, wrapped him in fine linens, and buried him in a new tomb he had recently purchased. Of course, we know what happened next — Christ rose from the dead on Easter Sunday and appeared to hundreds of people before finally ascending to heaven. The point is that Joseph had a significant role to play in the story of the salvation of the world. God knew very well that this rich man would be remembered forever for his splendid deed. What was God trying to say — at this most important moment in history — by entrusting his own dead son into the hands of a rich person?

After all, if God only loved the poor and wanted to glorify only them, why didn't he bestow this great privilege on someone with no money?

Very simply, God honored Joseph of Arimathea because, as a rich man, he was the *right* man for the job. No one but a rich man could have gained access to the Roman governor so quickly. No one but a rich man could have convinced the governor to hand over Christ's body so easily. No one but a rich man could have afforded a big new sepulcher in which to lay the body of Jesus. In other words, no one but a rich, successful, business-savvy man could have taken care of all the details relating to Christ's death and burial so efficiently and with so much "dignity."

The point is that money doesn't have to be bad. It doesn't have to be the cause of a person's damnation. In fact, it doesn't have to separate a person from the Almighty at all. On the contrary, money can be good — *very* good. It can even be a means of achieving holiness and bringing greater glory to God. And this is the key to understanding the relationship between God and the rich: it is always *conditional.* It is always based on an *if-then* statement: money will be a blessing to you *only if* you view it as a gift from

God; money will be beneficial to your spiritual welfare *only if* you are generous with it.

If you have this attitude, money can be a truly wonderful gift — both materially and spiritually. It can give you the power and the freedom to do so many things to advance the kingdom of God on earth. It can make it possible for you to experience so many of life's pleasures. It can help rid you of so much anxiety — which always serves to sap you of strength and energy. And yes, it can improve your quality of life to a remarkable degree and make the short time you have on this planet much more pleasant. To deny all this would be ludicrous.

However, if you don't have a godly attitude toward money, watch out. You may indeed accumulate a fortune in life, but you will be in grave spiritual danger every step of the way. Understand this well: It doesn't matter how many millions you amass or how big your mansion is or how much power you wield, if you don't use your money in the right way — in the way God wants you to use it — it will ultimately be a curse to you. In fact, the more money you have and use the wrong way, the more evil it will inevitably bring down on you.[14] All those biblical injunctions just *can't* be wrong.

Which brings us back to our prayer: *"God, outdo me in generosity."*

If you get one thing out of this chapter, please remember this point: There is a divine nexus between generosity and blessings from God. When my mother told me that I would receive two things for every one I gave away, she was really teaching me something very fundamental about God and the way he operates; namely, that *he will never be outdone in generosity.* When it comes to bestowing blessings, God will not allow a human being to do more than he does. When it comes to being generous, God simply will not consent to being upstaged.

In fact, this principle is so important to God that we are even permitted to "test" him in it. That's right — *test God.* The Lord, as you know, is always warning us *not* to test him. We've already mentioned that if you say the prayers in this book solely to see if God "comes through," they will automatically be invalidated. Except here.

There is one place in the Bible where God actually tells people to challenge him. There is one passage in all of Scripture where God actually uses the phrase "put me to the test." In the Book of Malachi, God asks the

Israelites to give him a tenth of what they earn. Then he says to them: "Test me in this . . . see if I will not throw open the floodgates of heaven and pour out so much blessing that you will not have room enough for it."[15]

At no other time in history did God employ such powerful words of assurance to human beings. On no other topic was God ever so direct in his promise to bestow rewards. He commanded us to "love our enemies," but he never guaranteed any earthly recompense to us for doing so. He told us to "do unto others what we would have done to us," but he never pledged any material favors or prizes for our kind actions. Yet when it came to the subject of generosity, God — for reasons that are not entirely clear — left himself wide open to challenges. In fact, throughout the Bible we see similar guarantees of rewards whenever God talks about the importance of giving to others:

- "Whoever gives to the poor lends to the Lord. Be assured He will repay."[16]
- "Give and it will be given to you, full measure, pressed down, running so much over that men will heap it into your arms."[17]

- "If anyone gives even a cup of cold water to one of these little ones . . . I tell you in truth, he will certainly not lose his reward."[18]
- "Blessed is he who helps the poor. The Lord delivers them from their troubles; he will protect them and keep them alive. He will bless them in the land . . . will sustain them when they are sick, and restore them from illness."[19]

The law of giving and receiving is as immutable as the law of gravity. It *must* work. If you are generous to others, you *will* be blessed by God. There are testimonies from people all over the world that bear this truth out — testimonies from people who were in dire financial straits but were somehow saved from ruin at the last moment. Testimonies from unemployed men who suddenly found high-paying jobs; testimonies from women buried under credit card debt who unexpectedly received tax refunds in the mail; testimonies from young couples who were inspired to start businesses that became instant successes; testimonies from people who were already successful and, who, for reasons having nothing to do with business skill, were able to parlay their small savings into fortunes.

What did all these "lucky" people have in common? What did they do to deserve such unexpected and undeserved financial blessings? Just this: At some point — probably right in the midst of their own financial struggles — they reached into their pockets and helped someone even less fortunate than themselves. Whether it was money, hospitality, or some kind of service, they gave of themselves — even though they couldn't afford to — and God paid them back, royally.

One typical story: The head of a small, not-for-profit organization I know recently told me about how his group had struggled for years to pay their basic utility bills. At one point, they owed $100,000 but had only $20,000 in the bank. They basically needed a miracle to get through the rest of the month. My friend was at his wits' end when the pastor of his church told him to try being generous for a change, instead of simply begging everyone for money. He suggested that the organization give a small donation to the poor. Though he had no idea where he would get the extra funds, as a desperate measure he sat down and made a list of ten charities similar to his own and sent each a check for $200. The total amount of his gift was $2,000. Sure enough, two weeks later he received an unsolicited check in the mail from someone who happened to see his group's newsletter lying on a table in the back of a church. The donation was for $50,000! Ever since then, the organization has regularly made contributions to other charities and has grown steadily and substantially.

Why did this happen? An atheist would scoff and say it was a mere coincidence. But the truth, once again, is that God will never be outdone in generosity.

Does this mean that if you donate $2,000 to some charity, you are automatically going to get $50,000 in next week's mail? Of course not. Before you rush out and start employing this prayer as a kind of quasi-investment strategy, let me try to clarify a few points. Indeed, we said earlier that it was important to proceed with utmost caution in this discussion because there are so many ideas here that can be misinterpreted. Case in point: Before me on my desk is an advertisement from a so-called Christian group that "guarantees" it can show you how to increase your net income "tenfold" as long as you follow a few simple rules. All that is required is that you "plant" a certain amount of "seed money" by giving it away. Then, through prayer, you simply "claim" ten times that amount from God. Once the "transaction" is cleared in heaven, God will send your money back to you, right away, multiplied by ten. If you donate $5, for example, God will give you $50. If you donate $500, the return on your investment will be $5,000. Easy!

The ad claims that this approach to investing is merely the "Law of Sowing and Reaping" put into action, and that if you follow all the recommended steps, you will "unlock the door to infinite riches." It even comes with a "30-day guarantee" (I'm not making this up) and asserts that there is "no risk involved whatsoever." At the bottom of the ad, in boldface type, is an invitation to send a tax-deductible donation to the group — presumably to jump-start your investment, and also as proof to God that you are serious. Of course the ad is sprinkled with biblical quotes and mentions the name of Jesus several times.

How do you think God feels about this kind of "generosity"? Do you think this is an approach to giving that he would support?

It doesn't exactly take a genius to see that this financial "program" is quite contrary to the prayer we've been talking about. God, the Almighty creator of the sun, the moon, and the stars, is not about to lower himself to become your stockbroker! Indeed, the whole idea of a structured, no-risk plan is contradictory to the spirit of what God is trying to do here. What God wants to instill in us is a pure, giving heart. He wants us to be able to share without thinking, lend without calculating, and give without counting the costs. He wants so much for us to adopt this generous attitude that he is even willing to engage in a little playful competition with us to see who can give more. It would actually be more accurate to think of this prayer as a sort of game we are permitted to play with God — a game of divine "one-upmanship." At first glance, it might seem that God is allowing us to "test" him, but in reality what he is really trying to do (and very slyly at that) is to *challenge us* to be like him. Of course there's no ironclad guarantee that God will bless you with cold hard cash — tens and twenties preferred. No one can tie God's hands in that manner. He's free to bless you in any way he likes, including in ways that don't involve money. But the fact is that very often he will do exactly that.

It all comes down to mind-set — or in theological terms, "purity of intention." Purity of intention has an important bearing on any discussion about spirituality and money. Your intentions will determine whether God will answer this prayer or laugh at you for saying it! The Lord, of course, would never laugh at anyone who prays sincerely. But there are some people who are not sincere at all when it comes to giving, insofar as they only *pretend* to be generous. Before we end this chapter, we have to briefly examine this phenomenon, because it's actually very common.

"Pretending" to be generous can take many forms. The first is the most familiar. You've heard the expression that when you give alms, you shouldn't "let your left hand know what your right is doing"? Well, there are some people out there who violate this guideline to such a degree that it's highly questionable whether they're generous at all. Indeed, some "philanthropists" couldn't care less about the people or the causes they give to. They seem to be interested in only one thing — getting the credit. Whether they're Hollywood movie stars who only want their names and pictures in the papers, heads of corporations who only want tax write-offs, or average middle-class men and women who want to blab about their good deeds so that everyone thinks they're wonderful people — none of them are being generous in the way that God wants them to be. I'm not saying these folks are bad, or that their donations are worthless. Nor am I saying that it's wrong for a person to feel good about himself after giving money away. That's a natural, healthy emotion put there by God, and a natural benefit he gives us because he *wants* us to enjoy giving. Hardly anybody is able to perform virtuous actions with complete purity of intention. Our motives are always mixed — God understands that. No, what I mean is that people who make donations *primarily* to help themselves are not fooling God in any way. Their reason for giving is to receive worldly accolades, not heavenly ones. Thus they shouldn't expect the prayer we've been discussing to work for them. As the Gospel says, "they have their reward."[20]

Then there are those who give away a great deal of money, but the amount is only a tiny fraction of their overall wealth. This, too, counts for little with God. These people might look, act, and sound generous, but in reality they're quite cheap! What they're basically doing is making "safe" donations. And safe donations, while praiseworthy, are not the kind God ordinarily blesses. Remember the widow's mite?[21] The moral of that story was that a person who makes a small salary — say, minimum wage — but who donates $25 every week has actually given away more *in the eyes of God* than a rich person who gives away $1 million! We must always keep in mind that generosity is a relative term. God judges us not according to the exact dollar amount of our donations, but on the amount of ourselves we invest in those donations.[22] The rule is that we are always called to give from our need, and not from our abundance.[23] That means that there are going to be times when it *hurts* to give our money away; times when we would much rather keep it; times when we might be frightened to give, perhaps for legitimate reasons. It's at those times that God will be watching us closely to see what we do — watching us to see if we have the strength to trust in him and do the right thing. *That* is the kind of giving that God blesses.

Finally, there is the biblical exhortation to be good "stewards" of our money. That means we have to be responsible as well as generous. Spending wildly on credit cards, for example, even if we might be buying gifts for other people, never qualifies as true generosity — because we're spending funds we don't really have. Nor is it being generous to give away our whole paycheck the same week our rent is due. We should never attempt to help the poor by depriving our own family.[24] We must always take care of our God-given responsibilities *first*, before we take on the responsibility of supporting strangers. However — and this is a big however — this doesn't mean we shouldn't try to do *both*. Too often the requirement to be a "good steward" is used as a rationalization by people who just want to be stingy.[25] "I can't afford to give $200 to this charity," they say, "because my kids have to go to college in a few years." Sorry, but that excuse doesn't hold water with God. You can always afford to give *something* away — and that something should *always* be more than you can afford. It's just that you shouldn't be so extreme in your giving that it's impossible to fulfill your other legitimate responsibilities. You should never be reckless.

These are just a few of the parameters that separate true generosity from "pretend generosity." It's important always to keep them in mind, but they should never stop you from embracing, wholeheartedly, the attitude God wants you to have about money. And that attitude, in a word, is *to give, and to give, and to give.* It's really not my purpose here to lay out any kind of systematic scheme of giving, or to impart any advice regarding what percentage of your income you should donate to charity (although tithing is probably the *least* anyone should do). The point of this chapter is merely to help you grasp the basic concept of godly generosity — and to encourage you to courageously adopt it as a lifelong habit. Because if you give your money away freely and consistently — regardless of the financial position you happen to be in — God will *always* take care of you and your family.[26]

In fact, if you really catch this vision, money will never again be as great a source of anxiety to you. Instead, it will be a source of adventure. Every day you'll wake up and ask yourself: What person down on his luck is God going to send to me today? What worthy cause am I going to be asked to contribute to? How much can I give without being irresponsible? Who am I going to make happy this week?[27] And last: What fabulous way is God going to find to bless me for my generosity? As with every other prayer in this book, the end result will be that you will be taken to a whole new level in your relationship with God. Soon you won't even be asking God to "bless you" for being generous. You'll be so grateful for everything else that he's giving to you that any material reward will be just icing on the cake.

The amazing thing is that you don't even have to be religious for this principle to work. Often people who aren't far along in their spiritual lives manifest a very pure willingness to give. God rewards them anyway — probably as an incentive to draw them in closer to him. For example, the well-known singer Frank Sinatra — who didn't exactly have a saintly reputation — was an incredibly generous man. He amassed a fortune in his lifetime, but it was also reputed that he gave away over a billion dollars to charity — much of it secretly. When asked why he thought he was able to make so much money over such a long period of time, even when he was well past his prime, he responded: "I don't know why, but every morning God just seems to throw money at me. All I do is try to throw it back! It's been working for years."

Exactly right! This is the true dynamic of sowing and reaping — and it is extremely effective. Whether you're rich or poor, sinful or saintly, up to your eyeballs in debt or rolling in dough, all you have to do is say this prayer and then do your best to be as generous as possible to anyone and everyone who comes your way. After that, just sit back and try to listen to what God tells you. It might be that he gives you an idea to start a business; it might be that he whispers in your boss's ear to give you a raise; it might be that he inspires your long-lost relative to leave you a fortune in his will! Who knows? Remember, God has *a lot* of money.[28]

So stop worrying so much about your bankbook! It's the easiest thing in the world for God to make a deposit in your account. If you have any doubts about this, just go ahead — test him.

4
I Can't Take It Anymore!
GOD, GET ME THROUGH THIS SUFFERING

A few years ago I went into an art supply store to buy a gift for someone, and I got to speaking with the owner. It wasn't a busy store — he evidently ran it by himself — and he was very chatty, asking me all kinds of questions about who I was and what I did for a living. I figured he was just lonely for company and wanted to talk. So I told him about myself, and about the fact that I was starting in as a writer, and that even though I didn't have an agent or an editor or a publisher of any kind, I was working on a book about heaven that I hoped might help people someday. The moment I mentioned heaven something very interesting happened. The smile on the old man's face disappeared and his mouth twisted into a nasty scowl. He abruptly turned his face away from me and said: *"Ahhch . . . heaven. Right. Sure."*

Of course I was surprised by his reaction,

and said to him, "I'm sorry — did I say something wrong?"

"Heaven?" he snarled. "Give me a break, there is no heaven. And God doesn't exist either."

"Well, I'm sorry you feel that way," I said. "But there *is,* and he *does.*"

"Listen," the man said. "You seem like a nice kid. But there is no God. And if there was, I'd like to meet him — *so I could spit in his face.*"

The old man then proceeded to tell me about some of the tragedies that had occurred in his life. There were many. His parents had died when he was a teenager, his brothers and sisters had died young — all from cancer — he'd lost several businesses, his wife had just passed away the year before, leaving him basically alone. The one remaining child he had — a son who never called him — was a total waste and had made a mess of his life. But by far the worst thing that had ever happened to him was the death of his daughter twenty-five years ago. She was a little girl — only eight years old — and she had collapsed suddenly one day while playing with her friends in the front yard of the house. She died in the ambulance on the way to the hospital. The doctors thought it might have been some kind of heart arrhythmia, but they were never really sure. Her death had devastated the man, and any vestiges of faith he might have had were ripped away, completely and irrevocably.

I listened as the old man related all this and I tried to think of something to say. But of course, there is never anything. I told him I was sorry for all the pain he had gone through, but I could see I wasn't doing any good. It would have been pointless to tell him about my own tragedies, or how I had been sustained by my faith, or how I was sure that, no matter what he thought, he would see his daughter again one day. But the mere mention of such "nonsense" as heaven had been enough to put him in a bad mood for the rest of the day, so I just left.

Unfortunately, there are no short, neat answers to the question "Why do people suffer?" There are no ready-made sound bites you can rattle off to people to alleviate their pain — not if their pain is great. That's why so many well-meaning folks end up saying exactly the wrong thing (albeit unintentionally) to their friends and family who are grieving over a loss. They say things like: "I know just what you're going through," or "Don't worry, it's all for the best," or "It's God's will," or "At least you had all those years together," or "You've got to stop crying and start living again."

Platitudes such as these, no matter how well intentioned, can feel like stab wounds to a person who is suffering. And it doesn't matter how true what you say may be. It might indeed be accurate to say that it was "God's will" for your grandmother to die; it might very well turn out to be the "best thing in the world" that you lost your job. But what does any of that matter when you are experiencing such emotional agony?

The thing so many people forget is that suffering is like an open wound — a bloody, gaping, open wound. And it has to be treated as such. The last thing we need to hear when we have any kind of traumatic injury is the physiological explanation for why tissues tear, or why we bleed, or the medical process behind platelet clotting. What we need at that moment is for a competent doctor to stop the hemorrhaging and bandage the wound so it can heal. If the doctor suddenly started spewing out all kinds of details about bruises and lacerations — as we were screaming in pain — we wouldn't gain much comfort from him, would we?

It's the same as if you were driving

through a fierce storm at night. As the rain pelts the windshield and the lightning flashes across the sky, obscuring your vision; as the sound of the thunder and pouring rain and windshield wipers going back and forth make it practically impossible to think — as all this is happening — what is the best thing for you to try to do? Would it help very much, at that moment, to attempt to understand where storm clouds come from? Or why different weather masses converge and produce precipitation? Or what the various scientific reasons for lightning are? What good would any of this information do when you are in the middle of a storm?

No, the best thing to do when you're in that kind of situation is to concentrate on holding the steering wheel steady, controlling the speed of your vehicle, and keeping your eyes peeled for turns in the road and for other traffic. In other words, the best thing to do is focus your energy on *getting through* the storm. There will be time enough later to figure out why you got caught in the bad weather, or — if you're interested — to take up the study of meteorology. But while the storm is actually raging, the most important thing to do, always, is to make it through, safe and intact.

God understands this concept well. Very often the last thing he will do when we are suffering is to tell us the *reasons* for that suffering. That's something he saves for later — sometimes much later. What he will always do, however, is help us to endure the terrible pain of the open wound; to make it through the storm in one piece. We'll talk more about the "why" of human suffering in a moment. But for now, let's understand this one point: No matter who you are or what your situation, God will always say yes to this prayer: *"Please get me through this suffering."*

Now, there are many kinds of suffering we have to get through in this world. Some suffering is big and some is small. But every kind can be torturous in its own way — from toothaches to kidney stones; from migraine headaches to bouts of depression; from frustration at work to anxiety at home; from the sad, deteriorating death of the elderly to the sudden, shocking death of the young; from the grief that every son goes through when his mother dies to the unspeakable agony of two parents mourning the loss of their child.

God says yes to all who come to him for help and comfort when they are in the midst of such trials. Notice I did *not* say that he promises to stop the suffering, or prevent it from happening in the first place, or alleviate it in any way. This may be one of the biggest stumbling blocks to faith, but we have to face it, head-on: God allows a lot of terrible things to happen. He allows diseases to ravage countries, hurricanes to destroy cities, murderers and rapists to terrorize communities. Remember, he allowed hundreds of thousands of children to be gassed to death in Nazi concentration camps. So yes, he may very well allow *you* to undergo some form of suffering — maybe the exact kind you dread the most.

Just look what happened to Christ. The night before he died, he prayed to God that he wouldn't have to endure the bloody, violent death of a crucifixion. He knew very well how much pain he was going to go through, and he tried to get out of it: "My father," he asked, "if it is possible, let this cup be taken away from me." Christ — the second person of the Blessed Trinity — made a last-ditch attempt to avoid suffering. At the eleventh hour, he asked for a reprieve. But since he was the perfect son, he also added, "Yet not as I will, but as you will."[1]

We all know what happened. His request was denied. The Crucifixion went on as

98

vn son, how can
it he will be any
v much we pray,
ough some hor-

ter what kind of
ure, God always
a way out of the
n the utter, black
; can lead us into.
er is — a way out
i famous passage
e Corinthians, the
d "will not let you
strength. With your
you with a means
of escape, so that you will be able to endure it."[2]

Spiritual writers often use that passage to illustrate that God will never allow us to be tempted to *sin* beyond the point that we can resist. But it applies just as much to suffering. God always gives us an "escape hatch." No matter how great our inner turmoil, he always gives us an exit through which we can go to avoid being trapped. When Christ prayed that he be spared the agony of the Crucifixion, God may have denied his request, but he promptly dispatched an

99

angel to the Garden of Gethsemane to comfort him.[3] The angel stayed with the Lord and consoled him, strengthened his resolve, and essentially helped him to get through the deep emotional turmoil and dread he was experiencing.

That's the same model of assistance God employs with us. Our appointed sufferings may or may not be prevented through prayer — depending on the situation and on God's will — but we, ourselves, can always count on being helped, consoled, and fortified by God if we ask for help.

Everyone at one time or another has read the poem "Footprints in the Sand." Remember its simple message? A man dreams that he is standing on a beach with God, watching all the scenes of his life flash across the sky. Below each of the scenes the man sees two sets of footprints on the shoreline — one made by him, and the other by God. Looking at the entire span of his life, the man notices something disturbing. Beneath each of the scenes depicting the saddest and most painful events of his life, there is only *one* set of prints. The man turns to God and asks, "Lord, I don't understand. You're supposed to help people when they're suffering, and yet at those very moments when I needed you most, you completely abandoned me and forced me to walk alone. Why?" The Lord looks at him with compassion and says, "My son, don't you see — the reason why there is only one set of footprints during those terrible times of anguish in your life is because it was then that I *carried* you."

There's a reason that this poem strikes such a chord in people — we recognize the truth in it. It makes us recall the times in our own lives when the pain was just unbearable, when it seemed as if we were going to be overwhelmed and swallowed up by grief — and yet somehow we made it through. At those times, it really did feel as if we were being carried along by some power not our own.

I remember many years ago when my wife's uncle died suddenly of a heart attack. He was away with his friend on a fishing trip when it happened, and we got a phone call late at night telling us the dreadful news. He was in his forties and had a wife, two small children, and a close extended family. His wife, who had been informed of his death just a little while before us, was in complete, utter shock. For the rest of the evening, friends and family gathered at the man's house, after being wakened from their sleep just like us. I remember all the crying and groaning that took place on that frightening night. I especially remember the wide-eyed, numb look on the faces of the man's two children as they sat on their bed watching cartoons at two a.m., not quite understanding what was going on around them. The only person who wasn't told was the man's father — who was also my wife's grandfather. He was in his early eighties, and it was decided that it would be better to wait till daylight to give him the news.

The next morning it fell to my wife to tell him that his son was dead. How does a young girl give her grandfather news like that? The only thing I had to do was walk into the house with my wife and stay by her side as she carried out this grim task — but that was tough enough. I won't go into the details of what happened, of how the old man opened the door with a big smile on his face and then realized from the way we looked that something must be wrong; how he kept refusing to sit down; how he kept asking the same question over and over again in a high-pitched, cracking voice — "What's the matter, dear, what's the matter?" — as he nervously fidgeted with his collar; how he didn't believe what we were saying; then finally, how his legs went weak and suddenly dropped from under him. It was an awful thing to watch. What I remember most vividly, though, was my wife and how strong she was, despite her own grief. I kept wondering to myself, Where in the world is she getting the courage and grace to handle all this?

A long time afterward she told me how she was able to make it through that morning. Though she was not very religious at the time, she told me she had said a silent prayer to God right before she rang the doorbell of her grandfather's house. Only she didn't ask God for anything. She *told* him he had to do something for her. "God," she said, "I'm not going in there alone. You're coming with me. . . . You have to, otherwise I just can't do this." After she said that prayer, she felt a wave of peace come over her, and was able to go forward and do what she had to do without breaking down — without collapsing from the enormous weight that was on her own chest.

She was able to go forward for the simple reason that God was helping her. If today she were to stand on the beach with God, she would see that beneath that particular scene in her life there would be only one set of footprints.

And yet this is where the whole footprints analogy breaks down. Because although my wife was given the assistance she needed to get through that horrible ordeal, God didn't do it *all* by himself. Yes, he propped her up, held her by the waist, let her lean against his shoulders, and pulled her along as they walked together into her grandfather's house. But he didn't carry her completely. She had to do much of the work herself.

This is an important point to understand. We said before that God always gives us an "escape hatch." No matter how great our pain, he always gives us a way to make it through the storm with our mind, heart, and soul fully intact. But even with an escape hatch, some effort on our part is always required. We still have to reach up, turn the valve, push open the hatch, and lift ourselves through the opening.

What sometimes happens, unfortunately, is that people get into a pattern of *not* using the escape hatch God provides. They fail to reach out to God through prayer, even in their times of greatest suffering. Or they fail to reach out to the people God sends their way to help them during those dark days. If this becomes enough to a habit over a period of years, then it *is* possible for these people to feel overwhelmed and trapped when their moment of tribulation comes. In those cases, they may not see the emergency exit God has given them — even though it might be right in front of their eyes. They may sincerely feel that for them there is "no way out," that for them there is "no hope." And they may never escape.

What becomes of these tormented souls? They become irrevocably harmed, emotionally, psychologically, and spiritually. Their pain suffocates them — not for months, or years, or decades, but *forever.* Some people go through a divorce or a breakup and are never able to love again. Some people are paralyzed in a car accident and are never able to enjoy life again. Some people lose a close relative or friend and are never able to believe in God again. The saddest people are those who, depressed for one reason or another, turn completely in on themselves, lose all hope, and are finally driven to the loneliest death of all — suicide.

No one is saying that these people consciously or freely choose their fate, or that God is going to hold them strictly accountable for their actions. It all depends on the inner state of a person's soul — and only God can see that. Knowing how kind the Lord is, it is probably poor men and women like these on whom he bestows the most mercy. All we're saying here is that every one of the horrible outcomes I've mentioned *could have been avoided.* Even the worst thunderstorm doesn't have to result in a car crash. Even the cruelest death doesn't have to result in the loss of a person's faith. Even the most severe case of clinical depression doesn't have to result in a suicide. God always gives us a way out. It may not be easy, but it's always possible. God always says yes to the prayer *"Get me through this suffering."*

Now, once we do make it through the initial downpour of the storm, we might be in a better state of mind to consider the reasons why it occurred. And this is where we enter into the greatest mystery in all theology: Why does an all-good, all-powerful God allow suffering to exist?

Obviously we can't devote the attention that this question deserves here. It would take many books to do that. But we *can* say that one of the keys to understanding this mystery — indeed, one of the keys to understanding the human condition itself, complete with all its triumphs and tragedies, ecstasies and horrors — is that there is something terribly wrong with *life.* I don't just mean that it's hard or cruel or painful. That much is obvious. I mean that there is something fundamentally "off" about it. There's something about life that doesn't make sense — something that's wrong with the whole picture. And this idea that life is skewed in some way is very much tied to the whole problem of human suffering.

You don't have to be a great theologian to see this. Anyone who can appreciate a dazzling summer sunset, or a crisp, orange autumn day, or a magnificent symphony, or the smile on the face of a beautiful girl can see that these marvelous works of creation simply don't belong in the same world as a cancer ward, a hospice, or a cemetery. The sight of a wildly happy child opening his presents on Christmas morning just can't be reconciled with the sight of a little white coffin in a funeral home. It's not enough to say that the world is full of both good and bad things. That explanation simply doesn't suffice. The good things in life are just too good; the bad things are just too awful. They just can't be part of the same plan. C. S. Lewis put it best; he said that human beings instinctively know that the good things in life are *supposed* to exist, while the cruel, painful things are not. He said that somehow we know that "right" has a right to be there, while "wrong" has no right whatsoever.

This isn't something we can prove by mathematics or science. It's just something all of us — as a species — can feel deep in our bones. So many belief systems, both religious and secular, try to claim that death and suffering are just a normal part of life. What nonsense! They may be *facts* of life — and facts we have to accept — but they are neither "normal" nor "natural" nor "good" in any way. Christianity is the only religion that really addresses this conflict squarely in the face; it's the only religion that challenges this great, global non sequitur by asking the question "What's wrong with this picture?" And it's the only religion that tries to provide an answer.

The picture is wrong because *something went wrong.* Life was never meant to be this way. Something happened. Something at the very beginning went terribly, terribly wrong. And we call that something the Fall.

Back in the Garden of Eden, our first parents committed a great crime that rocked the world, a gross act of treachery against God, the effects of which we are still feeling today. We don't know all the details, but we do know that it was a direct act of disobedience that came about as a result of pride. The Book of Genesis says that Adam and Eve ate the fruit of the tree of knowledge of good and evil.[4] That sounds so innocent to us, such a harmless bit of symbolism. But what does it really mean?

It does not mean that our first parents wanted to taste an apple; it does not mean that they were thirsty for knowledge; it does not mean that they simply wanted to know the difference between right and wrong. These are misconceptions. Adam and Eve did not want to discover the difference between right and wrong. They wanted to *decide for themselves what was right and what was wrong.* They chose to reject God's laws and make themselves the law. By a prideful act of rebellion carried out at the prompting of the Devil, they tried to *usurp God* and *be God.* That was their crime.[5]

And what they did changed everything. In rejecting God, our first parents rejected and lost everything that came with being close to God. They lost eternal life, they lost heaven, and they lost the friendship of their Creator. They lost it not only for themselves, but for the earth, for all of creation, and for all their descendants. Their sin was passed on, almost as if by genetics.[6] And what they gained by leaving the protection of God's side was not freedom, or knowledge, or independence of any kind, but only exposure to the harsh elements of a fallen world: death, deterioration, disease, depression, weakness, loneliness, old age, and all the rest of the long catalog of human ills that have plagued mankind since time immemorial.

And that, ultimately, is the reason why the world is in such a mess today. God didn't do anything to us — *we left him.*[7] He didn't cause Adam and Eve to reject him, and he didn't cause any of the suffering human beings have experienced as a result of the Fall. Very rarely does God ever willingly, knowingly, or purposely make anyone suffer. He didn't cause that earthquake that killed thousands of people; he didn't cause terrorists to fly planes into the World Trade Center; he didn't cause my wife's uncle to have his fatal heart attack; he didn't cause that old man's daughter to die in her front yard. God doesn't sit around heaven like some twisted, all-powerful sadist, picking and choosing people to inflict pain on. In the final analysis, all of that carnage is the result of the Fall.

What makes people angry at God sometimes is that he doesn't go out of his way to prevent suffering, either — at least not usually. In fact, God almost never uses his raw power to manipulate people or events. Just as he didn't stop Adam and Eve from rebelling against him, so he doesn't forcibly prevent people from doing bad things today;

so he doesn't forcibly prevent natural disasters from occurring. That's just not the way he operates. That's not the kind of world he has created. Despite what certain anti-Christian philosophers have claimed in the past, the God of Christianity has never tried to force his will on humanity or "enslave" us. On the contrary, he has been the greatest proponent of freedom who ever existed.[8] While it's true that he demands obedience from all his creatures, in practice he "allows" us to do almost anything we want — no matter how much damage we do to ourselves and to others in the process.[9]

And yet this same God who is so extraordinarily "permissive" did not leave human beings stranded in a hopeless situation after the expulsion of Adam and Eve from the Garden of Eden. He intervened in a way that no one could have predicted. In order to make up for the sin of our first parents, he did something truly radical. Two thousand years ago, he became a man, in the person of Jesus Christ. Born of a woman, he walked upon the earth and lived a life of perfect, sinless obedience. And it was this obedience — even unto death on a cross — that finally made up for the disobedience of Adam and Eve.[10]

Aside from all its other implications, one of the most fascinating things about the death and resurrection of Christ is that it shows us, on a very basic level, how much God is willing to get involved in our suffering. Just as you don't have to be a theologian to recognize that there is something "wrong" with a world in which there is so much pain, you don't have to be a scholar to know there is something "right" about a father who is willing to sacrifice himself for his children.

This is really where Christianity shows itself to be profoundly different from all the other religions of the world. Islam, when addressing the question of suffering, speaks only about the necessity of accepting the "will of Allah." Judaism maintains that it's wrong to even question God about this subject, because God is so far above us. Buddhism and the Eastern religions preach a sort of total detachment from life — the idea being that if you don't love or desire anything, you'll be better able to deal with the experience of loss. Only in Christianity is suffering at the very core of its theology and spirituality. Only in Christianity is it acknowledged that suffering is so horrible and so wrong that God himself had to personally intervene. Only in Christianity is

the primary symbol of the faith a cross —
an instrument of suffering on which a man
is executed.

While all the major world religions speak
about the need to trust God completely in
the face of pain, Christianity adds something even more profound to the equation
— something startling, sublime, and even
heartbreaking. The God of Christianity not
only says, "Trust me," but he says, "Look at
me," as well. He says, "Imitate me."

We can all recall examples from our own
childhood of times when we didn't want to
do something, but *had to* because our
parents insisted. Maybe we didn't want to
go to school, or take our medicine when we
were sick, or be sent to our room as punishment for doing something bad. Sometimes
our parents explained why these unpleasant
things were necessary, and sometimes they
didn't. Sometimes they gave us reasons, but
we didn't fully understand them because
we were still children. I remember when I
was a little boy, I was afraid of the water,
and how my father took me to a public pool
somewhere in Brooklyn and tried to teach
me how to swim. I remember him telling
me not to be scared of putting my head
under the water, but how I kept shaking my
head, refusing. Do you know what he did?

He didn't just explain that swimming was safe, he said, "Look at me." And he dipped below the surface of the water for a few seconds. When he came up wet and smiling he said, "See, that was nothing. Now you try it. . . . You'll be fine."

This is essentially what God did for us when it came to suffering. Through the words of his prophets, and in Scripture, he told us the story of the Fall of man. But he knew that wouldn't be enough. He knew we couldn't truly understand the gravity of sin, or why it must inevitably lead to death, or how we ourselves were partly to blame for all the bad things that happen because of the crimes and sins and acts of rebellion *we* commit against God every day. He knew that we would have trouble accepting all this if it was only presented as a theological argument, and so he also said to us, "Look at me. I'll go through suffering too."

And he did. He became a man and went through every kind of human suffering imaginable: depression, loneliness, dread, fear, anxiety, physical pain, humiliation, persecution, derision, long drawn-out agony — even the feeling of abandonment.[11] Everything we have to face, he faced, too.[12] He even threw into the bargain the worst pain of all — the death of a child. For he

114

made sure his own mother was present to watch his gruesome end.[13] Not because he wanted to hurt her, but because he wanted the picture of suffering to be complete. He wanted to be able to say to us: "You may not fully understand the 'why' of suffering, but just look at me. I'm dealing with it too. I hate pain just as much as you do, but I'm going through it all so that you know everything will be all right in the end. You can have hope that despite how bad things may seem now, you'll eventually be okay."

And so he died for us, and in doing so not only redeemed humanity, but gave us the perfect example of how to deal with suffering.[14] Today, when we have to face pain in our own lives, we have access to all the strength, peace, and courage that sustained Christ through his Passion and death.[15] God makes that power available to each and every one of us. When you say to God, *"Get me through this suffering,"* he will actually take you by the hand and lead you through your pain. No matter what the crisis, he's willing to walk right through the fire with you, and make sure that you get to the other side without being engulfed and consumed in flames.[16]

How he does that will largely depend on your personality and your particular situation. Suffering — especially grief — affects people in a million different ways. For some, the best thing to do after experiencing a loss is to get right back to work. Others need to take a break and go off by themselves to sort things out. Some people process their grief best by talking about it to anyone and everyone. Others need to stay completely away from the subject — the mere mention of it is enough to cause them excruciating pain. Some people need a simple shoulder to lean on, or someone to hug when they get home; others need to cry and to cry and to cry — to cry to the end of their tears.

When you ask God to help "get you through," he will guide you to *your* best pathway of healing. If you need a certain kind of person to talk to, perhaps God will send him or her your way. If you need solitude and a period away from everyone, perhaps God will inspire your boss to give you additional time off from work. If you need something consoling to read, perhaps God will put the perfect book into your hands. If you have to face a grueling week of medical tests, perhaps God will give you an extra infusion of courage. Sometimes when a person is going through a particularly agonizing period of mourning — say, over the death of a spouse or a child — God has even been known, on occasion, to provide a sign that the deceased relative is okay.

Sometimes God may send people to you who *need* comforting themselves. As we've discussed previously, there is never any shortage of people who are alone, or sick, or desperate for kindness. Helping others is the closest thing there is to a "cure-all" in life. If God judges that you're ready for that, he may very well point you in the direction of one or more individuals who are worse off than you.

No matter how God answers this prayer, one thing is certain: He will speed up the process of healing and make sure you get through your ordeal with as little emotional, psychological, and spiritual damage as possible. And this guarantee doesn't apply to only the great cataclysmic misfortunes of life. It works for the smaller "slings and arrows" of daily living as well. You shouldn't wait for heart attacks or terminal illnesses or car accidents to ask for God's assistance. You should say this prayer when you have a toothache; you should say this prayer when your annoying colleague at work won't stop talking to you; you should say this prayer when you're stuck in a traffic jam! Whenever you have to face *any* kind of pain, you should say to God, *"Lord, please help me get through this."*

And he will.

Ultimately, the difference between believers and atheists is not that believers suffer any less — they don't — it's that they suffer and grieve *with hope:* hope that their pain will end one day, hope that God has a plan for them, hope that their suffering has meaning, hope that God will somehow pull good out of even the worst miseries and tragedies of life.[17] We're going to explore this subject at much greater length in Chapter 9. We're going to talk all about Providence, and God's will, and free choice, and the redemptive value of suffering. But right now it's important to focus on one thing — the willingness of God to help you through whatever pain you're experiencing. I promise you, if you make a habit of saying this prayer throughout your life, you'll never get to the point of utter desolation; you'll never end up in the position of that old man I mentioned at the beginning of this chapter — the one in the art store who had lost his daughter. No matter how terrible your anguish, you'll never become bitter, cynical, disillusioned, or unhappy. You'll never think of spitting in God's face.

The reason is that God always says yes to

this prayer. Even if your agony is so great you almost feel as though you're going to die if the pain doesn't subside — God will help you. He'll come and find you, lift you up by the arms, and carry you out of the darkness. For this God we worship has been there himself. He knows what it means to suffer. He knows what it means to die and be buried — and he knows the way out of the cold, desolate darkness of the tomb.

5

AM I A TERRIBLE PERSON?

GOD, FORGIVE ME

One of my earliest childhood memories is a fight I witnessed between a little boy and a neighborhood bully, back when I was growing up in Brooklyn. The boy couldn't have been more than ten years old, and the bully was in his mid-teens. I remember hiding inside the doorway to the apartment building where I lived, a little frightened yet mesmerized, as I watched the fight unfold on the sidewalk a few feet away. The bully started by pushing the little boy to the ground, and the boy began to cry. But instead of staying down — as most other boys his age would undoubtedly have done — something strange happened: his face got beet red, his eyes narrowed, his jaws and teeth clenched, and he let out a tremendous yell. He got up off the pavement and, to the complete surprise of the older boy, charged him, swinging his fists wildly. He jumped on top of the bully and tried to hit him, all the while screaming at the top of his lungs. The teenager, who was obviously stunned by the boy's reaction, recovered quickly. He viciously flung the boy to the ground and cursed him. But the boy was undeterred. The moment he hit the concrete he got up and lunged at the bully again, furiously swinging his arms and kicking at the air. The older boy punched him full force in the face and threw him down once more.

By this time, the little boy's clothes were torn, his knees were scraped from the concrete, and his face was wet and dirty with tears. But nothing could stop him. Every time the older boy threw him down he got up and charged him, screaming and crying in a delirious kind of rage. He must have been thrown to the ground seven times. But every time he went down he got right back up, crying even more. I remember watching his face intently, literally in awe of his determination. There was nothing that could keep him down. The older boy finally got tired of all the effort required to block the kicking and punching. He yelled at the boy in exasperation, "Would you just stop it and get away from me!" Eventually, the teenager gave up trying to resist at all and had to practically run down the street to escape, cursing and yelling that the little boy was crazy.

For some reason, the memory of that scene has always stayed with me. The picture of that pathetic little boy, dirty and bloody and crying and beaten up, continually getting up off the pavement only to be knocked down again, has served as a kind of grand metaphor for so many things in life. I've thought about it when I was down and out and needed courage to fight. I've thought about it when I was up against what seemed to be overwhelming odds, or when I felt tired and beaten and needed extra strength to go on. But what that incident has always symbolized for me more than anything else is the power of the next prayer we're going to discuss — a prayer that has everything to do with *perseverance;* a prayer God always says yes to, no matter how many times we say it, no matter how many times we cry out for it, and no matter how many times we get knocked to the ground in the process: *"Lord, please forgive me."*

Everyone knows that God forgives sins. Christians, especially, have heard the expression that Christ "died for us" so that "sins could be forgiven."[1] In the last chapter we went over some of the theology of forgiveness. We said that by sacrificing himself on the cross, Christ atoned for all sins of all people of all times, before and after him. By living a life of perfect obedience, even to the point of death, he made it possible not only for people to go to heaven, but also for our individual sins to be absolved and wiped out forever.[2] That is the universal belief of all Christians everywhere, and it has been for over two thousand years.

What you have to understand is that when it comes to being forgiven for the bad things we've done in our lives, the hardest part has *already been done for us.* Christ completed the work himself, on our behalf, a long time ago.[3] Our role in the process is relatively simple. The more we can grasp this fact, the easier it will be for us to rid ourselves of the guilt, shame, remorse, and accumulated emotional weight from all the past sins that so many of us carry around our necks like millstones.

Let's use an example to illustrate this. I don't know how many times it has happened to you, but on occasion I've been very absentminded and misplaced or forgotten my keys. This is particularly frustrating when you get home at the end of a long day of work and discover that you can't get into your house. Short of breaking down the door, there's nothing you can do except call a locksmith. When he finally arrives, he has to drill out the old lock and replace it with a new one. Then he gives you a new set of keys and you can at last get in.

Now, in that situation we can say that the locksmith made it "possible" for you to enter your home. He didn't do everything of course. After he finished his work and packed up his tools, he didn't carry you bodily into your house. You still had to open the door and walk through yourself. But that was the easy part. The locksmith did the tough work. That's why he can charge so much money. Without him, you would have been sitting outside for God knows how long.

The same is true when you have a headache or some other medical problem and have to take a pill of some kind. The difficult part — creating the medicine, packaging it, and prescribing it — has already been done by the pharmaceutical companies and the doctors. The easy part — putting the pill in your mouth and swallowing it — is what *you* have to do.

God uses this same process when helping us in our lives. When it comes to solving many of the problems we're having, he will invariably consent to do most of the work himself if we ask him. But then he'll also insist that we play a role, too. Sometimes this role may seem to be extraordinarily difficult — at least at first — but in comparison to what he is willing to do on our behalf, what we have to do is really quite simple.

In the case of forgiveness, after the Fall of Adam and Eve mankind was in a truly hopeless situation. Because of what they did, it was no longer *possible* for people to go to heaven.[4] It doesn't matter how holy the Old Testament kings and prophets were, they couldn't get into heaven when they died because the place was bolted shut. They had to wait for Christ. Abraham, Moses, David, Esther, Ruth, Solomon, all the great men and women of that time — they all had to wait.[5]

What did God finally do? He rolled up his sleeves and did the hard part of redemption, the part we could never do ourselves. He became a man, went through life without sinning, and sacrificed himself in order to make up for Adam's sin.[6] Then he rose from the dead to "prove" that it was all accomplished. Thus God "unbolted" the door to heaven, and all the good people of the Old Testament, as well as all the saints after them, were finally allowed to enter.[7] In doing this, God essentially played the role of locksmith — or doctor. He made it possible for us to get into our home; he provided us with the medicine that could "cure" death. That was the really difficult work. But God also insisted that we play a role in the process of salvation. And this is where there is so much confusion today. Because people really, truly don't understand how *easy* our role is.

In the Gospel, Christ says: "Come to me, all you who labor and are heavy laden, and I will give you rest. . . . For my yoke is easy and my burden is light."[8] Many people have read those words and said to themselves, "But how can that be? How can the Christian burden possibly be light? After all, it's so hard to avoid sinning, it's so difficult to obey the Ten Commandments, it's so impossible sometimes to love our neighbors, or to forgive people who hurt us."[9]

We all know how terribly challenging and demanding Christianity can be. So how in the world could Christ possibly claim that it was easy? His statement seems to fly in the face of common sense. And yet he said it, clear as day. What could he have meant?

The answer to the riddle is that while it's certainly difficult to live the Christian ideal and avoid sinning, it's extraordinarily easy — almost ridiculously easy — to be *forgiven* for our sins. All we have to do, in essence, is walk through the door Christ opened for us; all we have to do is swallow the antidote he gave us. And the way to do both those things is simply this: We have to be sorry and confess our sins to God.[10]

That's it! If you are really sorry about committing some sin — any sin — all you have to do is apologize to God, and he will forgive you. Period.

The hardest part of what I just said is not doing it, but *believing* it. People all over the world claim to be Christians and then fail to accept this one, all-important doctrine. Without the slightest bit of exaggeration, I can tell you that the whole Christian religion boils down to this belief in forgiveness. It's the reason Christ came into the world. It's the reason for the Crucifixion and the Resurrection. It's the reason that the church exists today, and why so many saints throughout the ages have been willing to die for their faith; it's the reason that all spiritual books (including this one) are written and read.

In fact, the reason that the movie *The Passion of the Christ* was so gruesome and violent was because it was trying to drill home this point. It was trying to show, in a very graphic way, that all the sins of all time, committed by all people everywhere, were paid for — ahead of time — by Christ, in one bloody, agonizing, unbearable act of sacrifice. Without the death and Resurrection of Christ, sins couldn't be forgiven. That's the bottom-line message of Christianity.

Does that sound too good to be true? It's not! Think of a football game in which every fumble is ruled a do-over. That's the way God views our lives. Every time you mess up, drop the ball, foul another player, or do anything "against the rules," the referee calls the play a do-over — as long as you are sorry and confess. No flags, no ten-yard penalties, no turnovers of any kind. Christ spilled every drop of his blood that fateful afternoon on Calvary for one reason — so that we could be forgiven anytime we apologize — so that we could have all our fumbles called do-overs.

A well-known Hollywood celebrity once said that he couldn't "buy into" any religion that claimed you could commit a great, bestial sin on Friday and then receive absolution on Sunday. Many people would probably agree. But they miss the point. *You can.* It's not hypocrisy. If you're truly sorry and confess, you can be forgiven, no matter what you do, no matter how often you do it. That's why Christianity, for all its sublime dogmas and rich theology, is, at heart, the simplest and most uncomplicated of religions. Christ said that his yoke was easy and his burden light for a very good reason. Because it is.

Now, various faith traditions within Christianity may differ on how God's forgiveness is *communicated* to people, but all of them believe that forgiveness is a fundamentally simple matter. Catholics, for instance, have the sacrament of penance — better known as "confession." They don't see going to confession as an alternative to the forgiveness of Christ. They too believe that it is only through Christ and his sacrifice that we are forgiven — but they believe that his forgiveness is imparted through a priest. Moreover they don't say a person can't be forgiven without confession, but only that the sacrament is an *added obligation.* They therefore differ in their belief about the relationship of God's forgiveness to the community of Christians, but not about the nature and cause of that forgiveness. All Christians everywhere believe that the hard work of redemption has already been done by Christ, and that our only job is to be sorry.

Are there conditions that need to be met for this "sorrow" to be legitimate in the eyes of God? Yes, but even they aren't that difficult. First of all, we have to acknowledge that we did something wrong. This doesn't mean that we have to pretend that we didn't enjoy whatever sin we committed, or make believe that we're not drawn to doing it again. We just have to admit that it was indeed a "sin" and have some kind of negative attitude toward it because we love God and regret that we disobeyed and disappointed him. After all, this is the same God to whom we owe everything, including life itself. Unless we're the most prideful and egotistical of people, it shouldn't be too hard to muster at least some kind of sincere contrition.

Next, we have to honestly want to try not to sin again. You can't commit a robbery, say to God that you're sorry, and expect to be forgiven *as* you're planning your next heist. You can't cheat on your wife, say to God that you're sorry, and then expect to be forgiven *as* you're on your way out the door to your next illicit rendezvous. That's called "presumption" and it doesn't hold any water with God. There's got to be some attempt on your part to alter your behavior. There's got to be a willingness to let God change you. There's got to be a firm commitment to at least try to act differently, to try to stop, turn around, and head in a new direction.

But once again, the key word here is "try." Human beings are weak. We fall constantly. Some people commit the same sin over and over again throughout their entire lives. God knows that. He's been watching human beings commit these sins for thousands of years. It's not that he's grown used to it. It's just that he's not surprised in any way when he sees you repeatedly falling. If there's a particular sin you're having trouble with and you commit it constantly and feel bad about it constantly, then you're probably going to have serious doubts about your ability to overcome it. That should *never* stop you from resolving to try not to do it again. You may feel in your bones that your resolution is weak — even foolhardy — but that doesn't matter. Any resolution not to sin again, no matter how unrealistic, is going to be accepted by God. Why? Because his yoke is easy and his burden light.

Finally, as most people know, there is a famous line from the "Our Father" that says: "Forgive us our trespasses as we forgive those who trespass against us." What that means, essentially, is that God is going to be merciful to us in the same measure that we are merciful to others. This is God's quid pro quo of forgiveness, and its importance should never be underestimated. We are required to forgive others, not just once in a while, not just when we feel like it, but *all* the time. And if we don't, we are going to have the same strict standard of judgment applied to us. Thus, if you are a very hard, callous type of individual who holds grudges and harbors all kinds of animosities against people who have offended you, you may have a lot to worry about on Judgment Day. But, on the other hand, if you are one of those weak individuals who is constantly falling into the same sinful behavior but are also merciful and forgiving to others, then, as Jesus said, your heavenly father will treat you in exactly the same way.

This isn't some sort of a trick or slick way to get around the commandments; it's a clear biblical promise: "Blessed are the merciful, for they shall obtain mercy." The fact that you will naturally start to become the kind of person who is able to obey God's laws *as a result of* trying to forgive others is a spiritual dynamic that God is well aware of. In fact, that's one of the reasons he made the promise in the first place.

Now, it's true that forgiving others can be difficult. Yet many people completely misunderstand the concept. They think it means we have to have warm, mushy feelings toward the people who harm us. They think it means we have to *like* the people who have offended us or our families or have been guilty of some terrible crime. They think it means we have to *forget* the bad things that have been done to us. Nothing could be further from the truth.

Forgiveness has one meaning: wishing a person the greatest possible good — which basically means wishing them salvation and heaven. If someone hurts us, we can be angry at him, we can dislike him, we can choose to stay away from him, maybe even for the rest of our lives. If someone has betrayed us, we may never be able to trust him again. We may never want our relationship to "go back to the way it was." And if someone has committed a crime of some sort, we can do our best to make sure he is prosecuted to the full extent of the law. God doesn't have a problem with any of that. But at the same time we are experiencing those "feelings," we must also, in our mind, "will" that the guilty person is ultimately reconciled with God and goes to heaven. This may not be the most perfect kind of forgiveness, but it will do. It's God's "minimum requirement," and he will accept it. What God won't accept is when we wish evil on a person or hope that he will be condemned to hell. God reserves that kind of judgment for *himself alone.*

Now, there are cases when even wishing a person heaven is difficult to do. It might seem impossible for a mother to forgive the drunk driver who killed her son. God understands when serious emotions interfere with our ability to forgive. And he's patient with us. In these special cases, the best thing to do is approach forgiveness the same way we approach other things in life that are hard to do — by building up to it, by practicing. If you want to bench-press three hundred pounds, you don't start out by putting all the weight on the barbell at once. You begin with a lighter amount and gradually increase the load.

If you can't yet find it in your heart to forgive some big, horrible crime a person has committed against you, start off with something smaller. Forgive the person who cut you off at the intersection this morning on your way to work. Forgive the nasty bank teller who gave you an attitude when you were cashing your paycheck. Forgive your father for making that cruel comment to you and treating you like a child. Work on forgiving *those* kinds of things, and you'll eventually find it easier to forgive the really serious offenses that people commit. The important thing is *to build up a habit of forgiveness.*

You see, God is very reasonable when it comes to the subject of forgiveness. He wants to forgive you, he's anxious to forgive you, he's looking for every possible excuse to forgive you.[11] But he also wants you to have that same forgiving attitude toward others.[12] It's that simple.

Some people might read this and think I'm being too flippant about forgiveness. They might think that I'm not taking into account the gravity and magnitude of sin; that I don't truly understand how sin can enslave a person, strangle a person, and destroy a person's life. Well, I *do.* I've been there. I understand how terrible sin can be. But I also understand the meaning of the Crucifixion. I understand the purpose of Christ's Passion, death, and Resurrection. And I understand that the only reason he suffered so much *then* was so that we could have it easy *now.* Christ already did the hard work of atonement for us.

Once and for all, you can believe that sin is the greatest evil in the world and that God hates it with all his heart.[13] You can also believe that this same God is ready to forgive and forget the sins you commit

135

faster than you can blink your eyes.[14] This is not a contradiction. It's a joyful paradox, and one that does not in any way trivialize the horror of sin.

A much more legitimate question is, if obtaining forgiveness is so easy, why don't more people ask for it? Why aren't great crowds of men and women flocking to God to apologize for their sins? I know Catholics who haven't seen the inside of a confessional since they were seven. I know Protestants who haven't said a prayer of repentance to God in decades. Why such reluctance to utter those two little words, "I'm sorry"?

There are many reasons. Some people have no idea how much God loves them and wants to forgive them. Some people know but can't bring themselves to believe it, because it's "too good to be true." Still others are afraid to confront the sinful things they have done in the past because they think it will bring them grief, sorrow, or guilt. Human beings will do almost anything to avoid pain. We work so hard to hide our own frailties and weaknesses. Anytime we identify something in ourselves that might bring us pain, we try to pretend it's not there, or cover it up, or disguise it. Just look at the extent to which people will go in order to hide what they perceive to be their exterior faults. Plastic surgery today is a billion-dollar business! People will do the craziest things in order to remove a little wart because it makes them feel ugly and insecure. Well, people go to the same lengths to hide their internal warts as well. But instead of having cosmetic surgery or applying a lot of makeup, they do something else — they build up defense mechanisms of all kinds: they live in denial, they use their egos to shield painful and repressed memories, they run as far away as they can from whatever they think might be a potential source of anguish to them.

The only problem with this strategy is that it doesn't work! In the end, these poor people wind up living a great big lie. Whatever it is they did in the past that haunts them now can't be covered up by makeup or plastic surgery. It's there, underneath the surface, growing, year after year, until one day it becomes so intense, so tangible, so outwardly visible, that it's impossible to hide any longer.[15]

What these folks don't realize is that they're not alone. We're all in the same boat together! I may not have done what you did, and you may not have done what I did, but we've all done *something*. We all have our

137

own particular weaknesses, our own particular wounds, our own particular sins. Yes, some sins are worse than others, but we all suffer from some form of internal "bleeding." Every single one of us is screwed up in some way, and every one of us is at least partly to blame for the problems we have.[16] Sometimes we don't realize that we have these internal wounds because we don't recognize the symptoms — failed relationships, broken marriages, depression, addictions and habits that can't be conquered, dependency on pills or drugs or alcohol in order to sleep, dysfunctions of various kinds, phobias, insecurities, and so forth. The list goes on and on. All of these are signs that something is wrong *inside*.[17]

Of course, there are always going to be some people who refuse to believe *anything* is wrong with them. They think they're doing just fine, thank you very much! They don't have any problems or wounds. They haven't committed any actions in their life that they consider sinful, or shameful, or cruel, or scandalous, or disgusting. They're not the slightest bit sorry or embarrassed by anything they've done, and they certainly don't need to be "saved." According to their way of thinking, what we're discussing now is just part of a gigantic, age-old Judeo-

Christian conspiracy to inflict guilt on the masses. But *they're* not going to fall for it. *They* don't need to be forgiven for anything.

Well, I'm sorry to have to break the bad news to these folks, but they couldn't be more wrong. Not only are they fooling themselves, but they're making their lives a hundred times more difficult and more chaotic. They truly don't understand the ramifications of their actions — or of their unrepentant attitude. They don't realize that so many of the problems they are dealing with in their life *right now* could be resolved easily if they weren't so dead set against admitting their spiritual shortcomings.[18]

What all these people fail to understand is that while seeking forgiveness might involve pain, the pain is not going to kill them. It's not some crushing monster. Whether it results from facing the truth about our past, or admitting how weak we are now — the pain will always be manageable. God makes sure of that. In fact, in the end, it really won't feel like "pain" at all, but "release." The moment you say you're sorry to God, and know in your heart that you are really, truly forgiven, you will immediately feel as if a great weight has been lifted from your shoulders.[19]

Remember the cartoon, *How the Grinch*

Stole Christmas? Everyone knows the moral of that story. After the Grinch took all the presents from the Whos in Whoville, he heard them singing for joy and realized that, no matter what he did to them, he couldn't ever stop Christmas from coming. Christmas, he discovered, meant a lot more than mere toys and presents. But did you know that there's another lesson in that classic children's tale? All those stolen bags of gifts that were piled so high on the Grinch's sled represent something, too. They represent the enormous weight the Grinch was carrying in his soul. When he finally looked inside himself and realized the truth about how greedy and mean and jealous he was, not only did his heart grow "three sizes," but the burden of all the weight he was carrying disappeared. It was as if there was suddenly no load at all on the sled, and he was able to lift it over his head and fly back down the snowy mountain slope, triumphant, into Whoville.

So many of us are carrying similar loads. So many of us are carrying huge sackfuls of unrepented sins on our shoulders. When we look into ourselves and admit our faults and finally come before the Lord in repentance, it's as if all that weight were suddenly, miraculously removed. That's the power of

this prayer. These three simple words —
"Lord, forgive me" — have the ability to
obliterate the weight of all your past sins,
lusts, thefts, adulteries, indiscretions, and
crimes.[20] This prayer may not be able to
take away all the harmful effects of those
actions, and in many cases you may still
have to make some form of restitution for
them, but all your guilt before God will be
gone. The moment you say those words and
mean them, your soul will be a clean slate
— a bright, new, shining, polished slate —
on which you can write anything you like.
You'll be free to start all over again, fresh —
even if you have "started all over again" a
thousand times before.[21]

It's so important not to misunderstand
the meaning of this chapter. I'm not trying
to be "soft on sin." I'm not saying it's wrong
to be disappointed in yourself when you fall,
or that you should be content with living a
life of continual, habitual vice. I'm not saying that you shouldn't always be trying to
improve yourself, discipline your will, and
change your bad behavior. You should do all
that and more. But at the very same time,
you can't be harder on yourself than God
is. In this crazy, decadent, hedonistic world
of ours, where temptation lurks in every
corner and any person, place, or thing can

instantly become an "occasion of sin," it's very easy to screw up! To deny this would be insane. You can't beat yourself up every time you do something wrong — especially when you have a God who *wants* to be gentle with you and is standing there with open, welcoming arms every time you apologize.

Remember, a good Christian is *not* someone who doesn't ever sin, but someone who repents every time he does.[22] That means that, ultimately, the definition of a successful life is one in which we repent *one more time than we sin.* We've got to impress that definition into our heads and never forget it. We've got to have an almost military fervor about repentance. No matter how bad the sin, and no matter how many times we commit it, we can't ever allow ourselves to feel beaten or demoralized. We have to have the same exact approach to sin and repentance as Winston Churchill had to war. In the darkest days of World War II, when the Nazis were bearing down with all their evil might on Britain, Churchill was able to urge his fellow citizens, "Never give in — never, never, never, never. . . . Never yield to the apparently overwhelming might of the enemy . . . fight on the seas and oceans . . . fight in the air . . . fight on the beaches, landing grounds, in fields, streets and on the hills . . . Never surrender."

Never surrender. Never! That's the message of this chapter, and this prayer. Just like that beat-up little boy I remember from Brooklyn, who kept being thrown to the ground but refused to stay down, we have to rise up whenever we fall and continue the fight. If we fall a thousand times — if we fall *ten thousand times* — we should muster the boldness to say to God:

Lord, I know I did something terrible, and I feel awful. But I'm not going to let it discourage me. I'm sorry. I'm going to try not to do it again. But if I fail, I'm going to get right back up and try again. I may break the world record for committing this particular sin, but I'm also going to break the record for repenting of it! And God, I promise to do my best to forgive everyone who offends me. After all, if you can forgive me after all the times I've disobeyed you, I can at least try to be merciful to others.

This kind of prayer is music to God's ears. He doesn't just like it, he *loves* it. Just as I watched in awe as that little boy on the sidewalk continued fighting, despite all the blows he endured, God will look down at you from heaven in genuine admiration as you persevere in your struggle, without ever losing faith and heart. You may sin grievously, time and time again, but he won't be able to do anything but smile as he pronounces his merciful judgment on your soul: "Slate cleaned, door opened, burden lifted, sins forgiven — *Do-over!*"[23]

TH
KI
GOD, G

One of the most ~~p~~
always says yes to is "~~...ace."~~
After all, everyone wan~~...~~ — peace in
the world; peace in our communities; peace
in our families; peace in ourselves. This last
kind of peace is perhaps most important
because if we're not at peace with ourselves,
then it's impossible to enjoy life, no matter
what good things we possess. We can have
youth, health, beauty, money, an amazing
job, and a wonderful family — but if every
day of our life is full of stress, then every
day is going to be a nightmare.[1] On the
other hand, if we are at peace, then we can
handle almost anything that life throws at
us.

I don't know about you, but I marvel at
people who can remain calm and cool no
matter what kind of storm is raging around
them. They're like sailboats gliding along
smoothly on a glassy sea. Sometimes people

s their nature to
ng they do is mea-
even the way they speak
has the power to rattle them.
nice to have that kind of gentle
ion, and I'm sure it's a much
thier way to live. But being a typical,
passionate Italian, I can't relate to it in the
slightest!

Most of us struggle with anxiety on a daily
basis. We live in a perpetual state of reaction
— reaction to the thousands of external
forces that act on us all the time: TV, radio,
friends, family, work, e-mail, bills, responsibilities, current events, carnal desires,
worldly temptations, the weather. We're
constantly being pushed and pulled in so
many different directions that it's hard to
stand still and keep our equilibrium.

So what do we do? We take prescription
medications to get rid of all the knots in
our stomach. We buy over-the-counter
products like Alka-Seltzer and Pepto-Bismol
to eliminate the excess acid. We drink
alcohol, go for massages, practice aroma-
therapy, pay psychologists obscene amounts
of money, and even attempt to twist our
bodies into pretzels in order to meditate!
We do all of this and more because we
desperately want relief from the strain that

comes with living in our tension-filled, pressure-packed society.

Yet despite such Herculean efforts, our lives remain engulfed with anxiety. Why? What makes calmness and order so elusive in today's culture? Why is it so hard, in the words of the 1960s song, to "give peace a chance"?

The reason, I think, is that people have a very mistaken notion about peace. They either imagine it to be an interior "state of mind" that can be "achieved" through mental practice and self-discipline, or they think that it's something that is completely dependent upon exterior events. In other words, they believe peace will come about by itself whenever "peaceful" conditions prevail, and that stress will come about whenever problems arise in life.

Both views miss the mark. Both fail to take into account one all-important factor — God's role in the "peace process."[2]

Think about the people you know who are truly at peace with themselves. I'm not talking about the ones who are gentle and easygoing by nature. I'm talking about normal, everyday folks who are familiar with life's emotional roller coaster and know all about anxiety and fear and worry and frustration and passion. Yet they've some-

147

how managed to find a way of making deep, inner peace a normal condition of their lives — regardless of the difficult circumstances in which they find themselves or the challenges they are forced to face.

We've all seen individuals like this: the man who is told he has terminal cancer yet is able to walk out of the doctor's office with his head up, ready to spend the time he has left being a source of strength to his distraught family; the teenage girl who is paralyzed in a car accident yet remains cheerful, funny, and optimistic throughout the painful process of rehabilitation; the couple who loses their home in a hurricane and then devotes every bit of their time and energy to helping their neighbors in the devastated community. Where in the world does this kind of strength come from? How can these people remain so peaceful when the world seems to be crumbling around them?

The answer, in a word, is faith. Most times when you see someone handling things with grace and calm in the midst of a terrible crisis, you'll find that that person has a strong faith and an active prayer life.[3] Yes, there might be an occasional atheist here and there who will display great fortitude in the face of adversity, but that's the exception to the rule. Increased spirituality almost always translates into greater inner peace; and the reason is that peace — real peace — is from God. It's a gift that comes directly from the Almighty.[4]

In fact, it goes even deeper than that. Real peace doesn't exist independently of God; it's part of his very nature. God, himself, *is* the fullness of peace. We see this truth expressed throughout the Bible. The very first action taken by God in the Book of Genesis was to bring peace and order out of chaos. "In the beginning," Scripture says, "God created the heavens and the earth." After that, he separated light and darkness, divided the sea from the land, and then finally brought forth all the various categories and species of life. The whole act of creation was accomplished in an extremely orderly way. At first there was nothing but a dark, formless void, and then — after God got through with it — there was a highly ordered, harmonious universe governed by physical laws.[5]

Later on, in the midst of all the bloody warfare of the Old Testament, we see God constantly granting peace, proclaiming peace, bestowing peace, and promising peace to his people. No matter how great the carnage and confusion, God's people always had access to deep, abiding peace.[6] In the New Testament, Christ promised the same to his disciples. "I leave you peace," he said to them. "My peace I give to you."[7] He did this because he knew full well how much they would need the gift of peace in the future. The first Christians were martyred by the thousands. Whole families were mercilessly fed to the lions and tortured in Roman arenas. Yet these men, women, and children were able to face their brutal deaths with the most amazing calm and serenity.

Near the end of the Bible we see yet another indication that peace and order are part of God's character. After the Crucifixion, Christ's body was placed in a tomb and covered with a shroud. Two days later the apostles discovered, to their amazement, that he was no longer there. When Peter entered the tomb on Easter morning, he observed that the burial shroud was separated from the cloth that had covered Christ's face. The Gospel of John then reports the following fascinating detail: "the cloth, which had been on the Lord's head, was not lying with the linen shroud but was rolled up in a place by itself."[8]

Think for a moment what this means. Jesus Christ, who Christians believe to be

God himself, didn't just rise from the dead and miraculously appear before his disciples. Nor did he just get up off the stone slab he was lying on and exit his tomb, leaving his shroud and facial covering on the floor. No. Before Christ completed his mission on earth, he took the time to roll up his burial cloth and put it neatly in a corner. That means that the very first thing God did after rising from the dead was tidy up!

It's such a tiny detail, but it means so much. Remember, this is the same God who separated light from darkness and brought order out of chaos when he created the universe. Of course he didn't leave his own tomb messy on the day of his Resurrection. He left in an orderly fashion because he does everything in an orderly fashion. He is a God of order and peace.

That's why it's so utterly futile when people attempt to search for peace without including God in the equation. It's just can't be done, because God and peace are inseparable. You can read all the personal development books you want, master every relaxation technique under the sun, and meditate till you're blue in the face, but if the peace you're trying to obtain is somehow disconnected from God's peace, then it's doomed to be short-lived. The moment anything really bad happens to you, you're sure to be knocked off balance, and your life will go right back to being chaotic, turbulent, and stress filled.

And that's where this prayer comes in. If you ask God for his peace, you won't ever have to worry about peace being a mere "phase" in your life; you won't ever have to worry about it being some false feeling of tranquility that vanishes at the first sign of trouble. God won't let that happen. When you say the words *"God, give me peace,"* he will immediately begin the work of building up a real, lasting peace in your soul — a peace that resides deeper within you than any of your shifting emotions, a peace that has the power to endure any crisis, any storm, any problem.

How long will it take him to accomplish that?

It depends. With the other prayers we've discussed in this book, it doesn't matter all that much what kind of person you are or what kind of lifestyle you're leading for the prayer request to work. You can be the greatest sinner in the world, but if you look up to heaven and earnestly say to God, *"Forgive me,"* he will — right there and then. You can be a liar and a cheat, but if you say to God, *"Please show me that you exist,"* he will

152

give you a sign that he is there, in short order. You can be a jealous, lustful, envious old coot, but if you say to God, *"Please make me an instrument,"* he will send some suffering people your way — no questions asked.

But this prayer — *"God, give me peace"* — is a little bit different. God will say yes to it all right, but the rapidity and clarity of his response are going to depend a lot more on your relationship with God.

Let's say, for example, that you asked God for peace but were at the same time embezzling tens of thousands of dollars at your job. Could God grant your request right away? What if you were in the midst of a secret love affair with your best friend's spouse? Could God give you serenity at that very moment? What if you gossiped and exaggerated so much that even you couldn't remember all the untruthful things you said? Could God instantaneously eliminate the worrying you're feeling about getting caught in your own lies? Of course not! As long as you're involved in those kinds of activities, you're going to have a lot of anxiety, fear, and guilt to deal with — and deservedly so! God is not about to make those emotions go away. They're there for a reason — to help make you want to change.

153

Is God still going to say yes to this prayer? You bet he is! But he's going to do it on his terms. He's not in the business of helping people live in denial. His "peace" is not some magical, divine anesthesia administered simply to make you feel good. It's the real thing. It's deep. It's lasting. It's wonderful. That's why when you ask him for peace, he's not just going to give you a Band-Aid when what you really need are stitches. He's not just going to help you cover up the problem, when what you really need is to treat it. God's going to give you peace, but he's going to do it by helping you restructure, rearrange, and rebuild your life so that it fits into his perfect plan. And that may take some doing.

You see, the kind of peace we're talking about goes way beyond mere emotions. It has to do with being in union with God. Ultimately, that's the definition of true peace. It's the awareness that, no matter what else may be happening around you, everything is going to be okay, because you're doing what God wants you to do. No matter what turbulent and stressful calamities may befall you in life, if you're "right with God," then you're always going to have access to him, and, therefore, access to peace, rest, and calm *in him.*

On the other hand, if you're "wrong" with God, it will be impossible for you to have a peaceful life, no matter how hard you try.[9] Why? Because God is the source of peace. If you're in rebellion against him, then you're going to be in rebellion against peace itself. It makes sense that your days are going to be filled with chaos, stress, worry, and anxiety. They have to be. Deliberate sin, by definition, excludes peace.[10] Therefore, eliminating the stress in your life depends, in large part, on how successful you are in eliminating any big conflicts you have with God.[11]

And, of course, that's not always easy to do. It can be hard to break off an extramarital affair once it begins. It can be difficult to stop lying, cheating, or stealing if they've become ingrained habits. It can be an arduous task to be selfless if you've spent years being selfish and self-centered. Sometimes we're just not up to the challenge of reforming ourselves. Sometimes we don't want to alter our bad behavior, no matter how much stress it brings us. Instead of rolling up our sleeves and trying to change, we attempt to stave off anxiety by "simulating" peace in other ways. We set up all kinds of false "accommodations" that serve to reduce our worry and tension temporarily. Essentially, we try to create a superficial peace because the real kind isn't available to us.

Let's use an example. Say one of the walls in your home is beginning to show signs of mildew. You have a choice: you can either get to the root of the problem by finding out where the water is coming from so you can plug it up, or you can work around the problem and just mask the bad odor and cracking and ugly black spots. You can give the wall a new coat of paint, for instance. If you do that, of course, you're not really fixing the problem. You're just postponing it. Sooner or later, the wall is going to crack again, smell again, and become blotchy again. Then you have the same choice. You can fix it or you can try something else to hide it. You might put a big piece of furniture in front of the wall. You might light some scented candles and spray some air freshener in the room to hide the musty odor. And when that remedy failed, you might even try installing new drywall in front of the old wall. The number of false accommodations you can make is really endless.[12]

Well, we sometimes do the same thing when it comes to our negative behavior. We construct all sorts of false accommodations to hide it from our families and friends, and even ourselves. The strategy works for a while, but eventually it breaks down. A man who cheats on his wife, for example, may be able to create the façade of a healthy home life if he buys a beautiful house in the country with a white picket fence. He may even be able to fool his wife for a while by bringing her flowers, taking her to nice dinners, and telling her he loves her. But not for long. There simply can't be lasting peace in a relationship where one of the partners is breaking a solemn vow instituted by God. Even if the wife never found out about her husband's philandering, there still wouldn't be peace for very long. Serious problems would begin to manifest themselves in other areas of the marriage. Cracks would start appearing everywhere — just as they inevitably appear on mildew-infested walls that have been covered over with fresh paint.

We're all guilty of building up these false accommodations. We're all guilty of painting over the mildew in our souls. The problem is that sometimes we build up so many false layers of paint and plasterboard that we forget what the original problem was in the first place! That's when things can really get tough. Because at that point the only thing God can do to help us is to come in and smash everything we've constructed![13] That's why the road to peace is not always so peaceful. In fact, it can get pretty bumpy. Changing your life in a radical way can be a painful experience.[14] And unfortunately, the situation sometimes has to get worse before it can get better.

Now, please don't misunderstand me. Engaging in self-destructive behavior isn't the only reason people experience stress. Not everyone who suffers from bouts of anxiety is guilty of doing bad things, and not everyone who wants to achieve peace has to rebuild his life from the ground up. There are plenty of folks out there who are good, faithful, godly people and yet have a tremendous amount of turmoil in their lives. A lack of peace does not always signify the need for repentance. There are many other factors involved — not all of which are tied to morality.

Sometimes people get "stressed out" because of illness, sometimes because of conflicts with friends or coworkers. Sometimes the reason is purely physical — lack of sleep, overwork, or bad dietary habits. Many times the anxiety we feel is simply the result of bad mental habits — like constantly focusing on the negative and not the positive — or having a faulty system of priorities. Just think about how much time we waste "sweating the small stuff," getting all irritated and angry every time the waiter doesn't bring over our coffee fast enough.

Then there are the millions of people who suffer from nervous disorders. When the brain's normal mechanism for reacting to a threat — the so-called "fight or flight" response — goes haywire, a person can experience all the symptoms of a "panic attack": fear, heart palpitations, heavy breathing, dizziness, a sense of impending doom, and so forth.

None of this has anything to do with obeying God's laws. It has to do with the fact that we are weak, erratic, screwed-up human beings!

Whatever the cause of the stress, though, it's important to know that this prayer still works. God wants very much to guide you to the best way of eliminating anxiety from your life. It may be that he helps you to reevaluate your priorities. It may be that he brings about a long-overdo reconciliation in your family.[15] It may be that he inspires you to start a program of exercising and stress management. It may be that he leads you to a physician who will correctly diagnose your panic disorder and prescribe the proper form of cognitive therapy.

It may just be that God tells you to stop

worrying! In the Gospel of John, Christ says to his disciples, "Do not let your hearts be troubled."[16] Saint Paul repeats that same order when he says to the Philippians: "Dismiss all anxiety from your minds."[17] These weren't just suggestions, they were *commands*. And since it's impossible to command your emotions, it should be obvious that peace — real peace — can't be based on your emotional state. The decision to avoid anxiety is just that: a decision. You see, God never commands us to do anything unless he also gives us the power to carry that command out. Therefore we can be sure that no matter how "stressed" we become, we always have access to relief. We just have to ask God to help us make the decision to dismiss anxiety from our minds, and that will pave the way for God's gift of peace.

No one can say for sure what form that gift will take. The point is that God — the source of all light — is only too willing to illuminate your own particular problem and to show you the quickest, most efficient pathway to healing.

The critical thing is never to confuse the "pathway" with peace itself. That's what so many people do — they think that meditation and deep breathing are going to bring about true inner serenity. They're not. It's true they may help to reduce some of the daily irritations you experience, but they can never be a substitute for the kind of peace we spoke of earlier — the awareness that you're "right with God" and the incredible security that comes from that knowledge.[18] It's sort of like when you rub your eyes to remove dirt or dust particles. You can rub them till they're good and clean, and you may indeed see better as a result. But you should never mistake the rubbing for good vision.

There's a famous story in the Bible that illustrates this point perfectly. Everyone is familiar with the fact that Christ "walked on water," but not everyone knows that one of the main purposes of the story is to teach people the true meaning of peace. I'm going to quote the passage in full now, because it has such a direct bearing on some of the matters we've been discussing.

When evening came, the disciples went down to the water. They got into a boat and started across the sea to Capernaum. It was now dark, and Jesus had not yet come to them. The sea rose because a strong wind was blowing. When they had rowed about three or four miles, they saw

Jesus walking on the water and drawing near to the boat.[19] They were terrified and said, "It is a ghost!" And they cried out for fear. But immediately he spoke to them, saying, "Take heart, it is I; do not be afraid." And Peter answered him, "Lord, if it is you, tell me to come out to you on the sea." And Jesus said, "Come." So Peter got out of the boat and walked on the water toward Jesus. But when he saw the wind he became afraid and started to sink; he cried out, "Lord, save me." Jesus immediately reached out his hand and caught him. "O man of little faith," he said, "why did you doubt?" And when they got into the boat, the storm ceased, and those in the boat worshipped him.[20]

This story, related in the Gospels of John and Matthew[*] and so rich in symbolism, condenses into a few short sentences all the main points I've tried to make in this chapter. Peter and the other disciples play an enormously important role here — they represent humanity. All of us are being tossed about on a stormy sea, and all of us must face a good deal of suffering and anxiety in our life. Yet, in the midst of the

[*] I have combined the two Gospel accounts here for clarity.

winds and the rain and the turmoil, God offers us something incredible — the gift of deep, inner peace. When Peter stepped out of the boat and began to walk toward Christ, he was miraculously suspended over the water. None of the elements had any power over him. Despite the strength of the storm, he was untouchable.

But what happened? Why did he suddenly start to sink?

Peter faltered for two reasons. First, he stopped walking toward the Lord. After getting out of the boat and advancing fearlessly for a few paces, he recognized where he was and came to a halt, petrified. It was at that moment that he lost the ability to stay above the waves. We do the same thing. When faced with the problems of life — and the stress that comes with them — we try to "manufacture" our own peace and security. Essentially, we stop moving toward God and try to "do it ourselves." But, as we've already seen, God and peace are inseparable. If you try to obtain one without the other, you're doomed to failure. The one critical component to possessing deep, inner peace is being "right with God." And that means trying to move toward him all the time, obeying him as best you can, and then repenting whenever you fall.

The second thing Peter did was to stop looking at the Lord. Instead of placing his trust completely in God, he turned his attention instead to the wind and the waves. That's when he panicked — and that's when he started to drown. Again, we do the very same thing. We can be sailing through life, relatively free from worry and pain, and then all of a sudden storm clouds gather and the downpour begins — and we're stuck right in the middle. The wind blows against us and the sea rises around us and it can be pretty scary. Unfortunately, there's very little that can be done to avoid such situations. Suffering comes to everyone.[21] No matter how smart you are, no matter how rich you are, there's just no way to prevent "external" events from interfering with your plans. That's why you can't ever allow your peace of mind to depend on external events. When Peter focused all his attention on what was going on around him, he took his eyes off God. He looked up, down, around, and sideways, and was quickly overwhelmed with terror. How could he not be? He was alone at sea in the middle of the night while a tempest was blowing. He had no chance, and he knew it.

How often do we act in the same fashion? How many times do we look at all the problems in our life and start to panic? Even when we manage to keep our composure on the outside, stress is busy eating away at our insides. It's impossible to be happy that way. The only solution is to keep your eyes focused on God. Only he knows your final destiny. Only he can grant you eternal happiness in heaven, and only he can give you true joy in this life. Therefore the more you are able to give yourself over to his will and "cast your anxieties" onto him, the more you'll be able to experience true peace, despite what may be happening around you.[22] This is what the saints of old meant when they spoke of "total abandonment" to God.

Now, it's very easy to oversimplify all this and turn it into a cliché. Sometimes well-meaning preachers and self-help experts do just that. They try to make this Gospel story into some kind of a you-can-do-anything-if-you-put-your-mind-to-it motivational talk. They try to claim that "problems only exist in the mind" and that as long as you have faith, or a "positive mental attitude," you can make all of your troubles go away. Well, I'm afraid that's not the way life works. Suffering, turmoil, conflict, and indecision are all realities, and we have to deal with them. You can't just pray to God and expect him to make all your problems magically disappear. That's not the way to true peace. That's only a way of avoiding responsibility. When bad things happen to us and to other people, we have a moral obligation to get involved. We have a duty to fight evil and alleviate suffering. We have a responsibility to look adversity squarely in the face and struggle against it with every fiber of our being. It's just that in our effort to deal with these external challeneges, we can't ever allow ourselves to focus on them to the exclusion of what's most important in life — our relationship with God.

When we make God number one in our minds, even our struggles can become a means of bringing us closer to him. And that, once again, is the definition of true peace: union with God. When Peter focused his mind, heart, and soul on the Lord, he was able to walk on water. But walking on water didn't mean that he could stop the sea from rising or the wind from blowing. It meant that he was able to stay above the waves and overcome the storm.

That's exactly what God is willing to do for us. He's willing to give us a peace that, in the words of Scripture, "transcends all understanding."[23] No matter what kind of stressful problems we encounter in life, no matter how aggravating the situation or terrible the suffering, we always have the ability to face our challenges with amazing calmness and strength of character.

If you doubt this, maybe you should try taking a short break from all the commotion and tension and noise of your life. Life is so very noisy. Perhaps you need to close your eyes and shut out the world for a little while. Try to forget all the problems, all the worries, all the details, and all the responsibilities that have been weighing so heavily on your mind. Try to place yourself, for just a few seconds, back in that dark tomb in Palestine, on that first Easter morning. If you could be there now, just before daylight, and watch the Resurrection take place, what would you see?

You would see the King of the universe — the person responsible for placing the planets in their orbits and for laying the foundation of the world; the person who was and is ultimately responsible for all the activities that have ever taken place, all the busyness, all the bustle, all the enterprise, all the movement, all the work, all the energy, all the power, and all the life that ever existed[24] — you would see that person slowly and methodically folding his garments and placing them in a corner, quietly making sure his burial chamber was in perfect order before departing it forever.

If you ask *that* person for some of his peace, you can rest assured that his answer will be yes.[25]

7
Okay, I Admit It: I'm Afraid
GOD, GIVE ME COURAGE

Did you ever notice that people are sometimes very willing to confess their shortcomings? They'll readily tell you that they're suffering from all sorts of physical or emotional
problems. They'll admit when they're
"stressed out" or "run-down." They won't
need much prodding to reveal that they
have a bad temper or a tendency to be self-
centered or stubborn. People will even
reluctantly concede that they're "not that
smart." But one thing no one ever likes to
admit — either to others or to themselves
— is that they might be "cowards." Nobody
ever likes to let on that they're afraid of
anything. Of all the human frailties, coward-
ice is by far the least "popular."

Most people, in fact, believe that they're
pretty brave. They don't think they need
much help from above when it comes to
courage. Well, even if you happen to be one
of these people, don't skip over this chapter

169

just yet! Fear is a very big subject, and this prayer, *"God, give me courage,"* covers an awful lot of territory. When you come right down to it, it might just be the most important prayer in this book.

Before we begin discussing it, though, I'd like to relate something frightening that happened to me many years ago. It sort of frames this entire discussion.

Now, I know a lot of people are frightened by a lot of things, but this particular experience was a little unique. I remember I had just gotten home from a date and it was late — maybe two or two-thirty a.m. Just as I walked in the door, the phone rang. Getting a phone call late at night is always a scary thing, and my pulse definitely quickened. But it was Father Frank Pavone, a priest I knew from my neighborhood parish.

I was in my mid-twenties at the time, and Father Frank had recently been attempting to get me involved in the church community. I had gone to him with some questions about the faith a few months earlier, and he must have seen something in me, because he immediately started asking me to take on various volunteer assignments in the parish and the parish school. But his call on this late evening had nothing to do with that.

Apparently he had tried to get me earlier when I was out. He sounded relieved to finally reach me. He proceeded to tell me a very strange story. It seems that there was a family in the diocese that was claiming to be experiencing some kind of "demonic" activity in their house. They weren't saying that anyone was possessed, but rather that eerie things were happening in their home involving furniture moving, strange noises and voices. They had reported this to the Church, and were requesting that an exorcism be done.

Now, the Church doesn't just "do" exorcisms. Even when the case seems genuine — and that is extremely rare — there is a lengthy investigation process that has to take place before anything official is done. Father Frank explained to me that he had met with the family on numerous occasions, and that while they seemed to be slightly dysfunctional, they certainly weren't crazy. There really appeared to be something unusual going on in the house, and that something merited further observation.

Since the supposed demonic activity usually took place at about three-thirty a.m., Father Frank had to be there at that time to see for himself what was going on. He told me that as part of the investigation, the

Church was permitting him to have one "lay observer" present, whose responsibility it would be to file an independent report to the diocese. The purpose of his call was to ask me if I wanted to be that person.

Now, to be honest, I've never been the bravest person in the world. I'm not a coward in any way, but let's just say I'm the kind of man who when given the choice between watching a funny movie and a scary one will pick the comedy every time. At the mere mention of demons, a chill ran down my spine. And now Father Frank was asking me to be part of some kind of "pre-exorcism" investigation.

I had to decide immediately, since it was almost three o'clock and Father Frank was due to be at the house. I said yes but wasn't happy at all. It was just too weird for me — the surprise late-night call, the alleged demonic activity, the need to leave immediately. Talk about something coming out of left field! I was only just starting to become committed to my faith again, and this seemed a bit much to deal with so early in the process. But what was I going to do? Chicken out?

When I arrived at the house, Father Frank met me in the driveway. He told me a little about the family and the kind of problems they said they were having. Father Frank was always very closemouthed about divulging any kind of personal information, but I could sense from the way he described the family that they must have been a little strange. We went up through the porch to the front door and were immediately greeted by the entire clan — a grandfather, two uncles, the mother and father, and two teenage daughters; all of them lived under the same roof.* As soon as they saw Father Frank, they took him by the arm and practically dragged him into the house, asking him to bless it and say some prayers. Father Frank obliged them by opening his Bible and reading from one of the Psalms. After this, we were quickly ushered into the kitchen, where we sat down and were told about the latest round of "activities" that had taken place.

According to the father, on the previous night, at precisely three-thirty a.m., his eldest daughter, who couldn't sleep, had seen a strange glowing light coming from a mirror in her bedroom. When she approached it, the mirror fell from the wall by itself and shattered into a hundred different

* I have changed a few details here in order to protect the identity of the family.

pieces. Immediately following this, the bookshelf hanging on the opposite wall tipped over, spilling all the books to the floor.

I listened to all of this patiently but was extremely skeptical. I've always had a strong suspicious streak in me, especially when it comes to reports of "supernatural" occurrences. After spending a few minutes with this family, I was beginning to think they might be the worst kind of superstitious Catholics. When the teenage daughter mentioned that she thought the glowing light in the mirror had begun to take the shape of some sort of "creature," I had to restrain myself from making a sarcastic remark.

Still, there was something very unnerving about being in the house. The whole family seemed to really believe what they were saying. And they weren't that odd, after all. Every one of them was either holding a responsible job or going to school — even the grandfather still worked. Could they all be seeing things? Plus I remembered reading somewhere that in actual cases of possession or demonic infestation, it wasn't all that unusual for the people under attack to be a little unbalanced psychologically. The Devil loves playing games with people's night, either.

Father Frank and I came back the following night, and all was quiet. Then a third night, and still nothing. I became more suspicious of the family than ever. Maybe they had seen me running around the house trying to expose their hoax and decided to give up their efforts to trick us. Even though I couldn't figure out what their motive could possibly be, I got it into my head that they were making the whole thing up. In my report to the diocese, I recommended that there should be continued observation but that no official measures be taken just yet, because there were still too many unanswered questions.

Though it might seem a bit anticlimactic, that's basically where the story ends. The family complained to Father Frank once or twice in the next few weeks about other unusual incidents, but things seemed to quiet down after that. As it turned out, they wound up moving out of state a month or so later, when a better job opportunity came up for the father. The new family that moved into the house had no problems whatsoever.

After all these years, I'm still not sure what to make of what happened that night. I think that if the same thing occurred today,

minds, and it's much easier to do that if a person is slightly off to begin with. Also the Devil is famous for making matters confusing. And since I was confused about this whole situation, I thought maybe he was just doing his job very well. At any rate, I was trying to keep an open mind.

At about ten minutes after three, everyone got quiet and just sat there and waited. The kitchen table was directly across from the bedroom where most of the "activity" had supposedly taken place. The door to the bedroom was wide open, and Father Frank and I had positioned ourselves so that we could see right into it. The house was dark and silent and eerie. Father Frank looked very serious. Despite my skepticism, I found myself feeling scared.

Then, as if on cue, at about a minute past three-thirty, as my eyes were trained on the bedroom, I saw a piece of paper blow off one of the bookshelves and float diagonally across the room and onto the floor. It floated down so innocently and quietly. Under any other circumstances, I would have thought nothing of it; I would have simply assumed that a breeze had blown the paper from where it had been resting. But because it had happened at the exact moment we were expecting, we all jumped.

Then there was a noise of what sounded like a book falling off a shelf. Father Frank immediately leapt from the table and raced into the room. Fear momentarily gripped me and I froze. Was this really happening? But seeing Father Frank rush in so confidently helped me to recover. I followed quickly behind him and couldn't help noticing that there was a smile on his face — obviously he was enjoying all this.

In a flash, the two of us were in the center of the room. We stopped there and waited, each of us looking in a different direction. I have to admit, by now I was frightened. Could there really be a demon in the room? And if so, how much danger was I in? Just then the unbelievable happened — the chest of drawers that was standing against the wall suddenly lurched forward. The entire bureau, which was about four feet long and three feet high, moved toward me a few inches, making a screeching noise as it stopped. I jumped back two feet and almost knocked Father Frank over. I exchanged a quick look with him that said, What the heck is going on here?

But interestingly enough, it was at that moment that all my skeptical instincts took over. Maybe it was a defense mechanism against fear — or maybe it was a sudden

burst of confidence because there was such a holy priest nearby — but I made an instantaneous decision that this was all nonsense; that what I was witnessing was not something supernatural but a ruse of some kind. The family was just trying to pull something over on us, and I was going to get to the bottom of it. I immediately bent down to the floor and looked underneath the bureau to see if someone had pushed the furniture forward. There was no one there. I checked the sides of the bureau, then the back of the bureau — then I checked all four corners of the room. Again, no signs of anything wrong. I ran out of the room and asked the father if there was a basement in the house. He pointed to the door. Without asking permission I raced down the stairs and tried to locate the exact spot under the bedroom. When I found it, I checked to see if there were any wires or pulleys or strings of any kind that could have been used to move the bureau from below. Nothing again. I was like someone trying to figure out how a magician performed a trick — but without any success.

When I got back upstairs, Father Frank was in the room praying aloud. Nothing further had happened while I was in the basement. Nothing happened the rest of the

I would be just as skeptical, but I would probably be more open to at least considering the possibility that something demonic had taken place. I've just seen too much genuine evil in the world to be a complete cynic about the Devil and his activities. And that bureau did move — of that I'm sure.

But you know what? The thing that stands out most in my memory about that experience isn't the fact that a piece of furniture lurched forward mysteriously. It's the contrast between how scared I was, initially, and how completely unafraid Father Frank was. As long as I live I'll never forget the look of glee on his face as he rushed into that room, his Bible in one hand, his cross in the other, ready to do battle with Evil. If there were demonic forces present that night, Father Frank was ready for them, and there wasn't a doubt in his mind that he and his God would demolish them.

Where does that kind of fearless confidence come from? If we were all able to access that sort of courage anytime we wanted, our lives would be so much easier — and happier. Most people don't realize it, but courage isn't needed only to confront danger — it's much, much bigger than that: Courage is the cornerstone and linchpin of the entire moral order.

C. S. Lewis said that "courage is not simply one of the virtues, but the form of every virtue at its testing point, which means at the point of highest reality." In saying this he was following in the tradition of Aristotle and Thomas Aquinas, who believed that all the virtues — if they are to be of any practical value — must act with a "firmness" that can only be maintained by courage. In other words, for a person to be honest or merciful or chaste or magnanimous or patient, he must first have the courage to overcome all the obstacles that stand in the way of practicing those virtues. At some point, strong temptations are going to present themselves. That's the moment when courage is most important. Essentially, a person must have the guts not to give in.

Courage — or fortitude, as it used to be called — is needed in life to do any kind of good or resist any kind of evil. You need courage to follow all the commandments, to face physical danger, to overcome fears, both rational and irrational. You need courage to struggle against neuroses and phobias, to overcome addictions, to persevere through life's difficulties, to endure suffering. You need courage to take risks, to give witness to the truth, to dare to do great things. In short, you need courage for just about everything. That's why Churchill wrote that "courage is rightly considered the foremost of virtues, for upon it all others depend." And why Franklin Roosevelt said "the only thing to fear is fear itself." Both of these leaders understood the all-encompassing importance of courage.

And that's why we're so unbelievably fortunate that God always says yes to the prayer *"Please give me courage."* Did you know that in virtually every book of the Bible God tells us to be brave? In fact, the words "fear not," "be not afraid," or variations on that phrase appear 144 times in sacred Scripture![1] And they aren't just suggestions — they're commands. The Bible doesn't say, "Try not to be afraid," it says, "Don't be afraid." It doesn't say, "Do your best to be strong," it says, "Be strong and fear not, for I will help you." As we've said previously, God never gives a command unless he also gives us the ability to follow that command. For example, he doesn't expect everyone to become pastors or priests, because he doesn't give everyone the ability to perform those roles. He doesn't require everyone to write books about the faith or preach sermons about it, because he doesn't give everyone the ability to carry out those tasks. But he does command everyone to have courage. Why? Because he gives everyone the ability to overcome the fears they have to face in life.

You see, courage isn't just a skill or a talent or an ability that human beings possess. It's a gift.[2] Yes, a person can have a fearless disposition, in the same way that some people are born with gentle and peaceful natures. But the kind of courage we're talking about here is much more than that — it's something that is added onto our personality. Thomas Aquinas used the famous theological expression "grace builds on nature" to describe the phenomenon. What it means is that God can take what we are born with, or what we have acquired in life by observation or habit, and then infuse even more of it into our souls, supernaturally. Basically, he can inject us with a special, divine "shot" of courage anytime he wants.

Let's say that you have to give a talk to a group of people and are very nervous about it. It's been said that the fear of speaking in public is one of the greatest fears in the world. Well, when it comes time for you to make your speech, you might be petrified; you might be on the verge of canceling out, playing sick, or leaving town! But if you

182

were "right with God" (as we discussed in the last chapter), or at least trying to get right with him, and you asked him for courage, there is no doubt that God would give you an extra measure of bravery at that moment.[3] You might still be scared — you might still be sweating right up till the time you started speaking — but you'd be able to go through with it. God would say yes to your prayer and you would be okay. You would not fall flat on your face.

We all have different natural talents and skills. Some people have an easy time with public speaking — they're just hams by nature. If they have to give a speech, they don't need as much "extra" help from God. Maybe you need more grace to build on your nature than they do. Likewise, some people don't have to think twice when it comes to taking dangerous chances. If they see a building on fire, they might just rush into it in order to save the occupants, without giving a second thought to the risks involved. Other people wouldn't even consider doing that — there's just no way they would take a chance on being gravely injured or losing their life.

The point is that the second kind of person — the one who is not naturally inclined to physical bravery — has the ability to take the very same courageous action as the person who is by nature inclined to be brave — as long as he or she asks God for help. God has the power to even everything out. He has the power to help that person act just as bravely as the person who is fearless by nature. We've all seen cases of this, when a man or woman who is small, weak, timid, and frail turns out to be the bravest of heroes. In fact, the overwhelming number of people who have won the Congressional Medal of Honor do not look and act like John Wayne. What accounts for this? Very simply, God is willing to distribute massive doses of supernatural grace to those of his children who are rightly disposed to him, and who ask for courage.[4]

This doesn't happen only in instances of physical danger, either. It applies to every situation that requires courage. When Mother Teresa first began ministering to lepers in Calcutta, she couldn't help being overcome with disgust. She literally spent weeks vomiting. She just didn't have a natural inclination to deal with all the filth and squalor around her. But she prayed to God for courage. What happened? In a short time she was kissing those same lepers; she was embracing them, loving them, showering them with genuine affection. God had given her divine graces that made it possible for her to overcome all her natural impulses of loathing.

The same was true of the apostles. Remember how they acted during the Passion? They deserted Christ, denied him, and ran as far away from him as they could.[5] And this was after they had seen him raise people from the dead! This was after they had seen him walk on water, calm storms, multiply loaves and fish, exorcize demons, and perform countless miracles. Of course they didn't really understand what was going on and they were afraid of being crucified themselves. But what was their excuse after the Resurrection — after Jesus actually rose from the dead? What was their excuse after they saw him alive again, in his glorified body? That's when they saw him actually walk through walls! They spent over a month with him and witnessed many incredible miracles before he finally ascended to heaven.[6]

You would think that after that experience — after they saw with their own eyes that even death couldn't overcome him — they would finally have the courage to face their own persecution. But did they begin preaching or healing or spreading the good news about Jesus? No. They hid in the "upper room" by themselves. They cloistered themselves away from everyone. They prayed and waited. It wasn't until after Pentecost Sunday when the Holy Spirit came down upon them that they went out and began the work of spreading the Gospel. In the final analysis, it wasn't the miracles that made the apostles fearless, nor was it hearing the message of salvation proclaimed to them, or even spending time with the Lord. No — it was a freely bestowed gift of the Holy Spirit. The moment they received courage from God, they immediately left their hiding place, went outside, and began taking chances and facing danger.

We talked in the last chapter about how difficult it can sometimes be to stop negative behavior — to sever extramarital relationships, to stop lying or gossiping, to break bad habits. Anytime a person wants to change it's hard. That's where this extra dose of courage comes in so handy. We're all so set in our ways. Aside from the obvious reasons, we've always got inertia to contend with. Remember the principle of inertia? An object at rest has a tendency to stay at rest. Well, that's true when it comes to everything in life, not just physical bodies. It's just hard for us to take any kind of action that we perceive to be either difficult or painful. The ironic thing is that once you take those first few painful steps, everything gets very easy, very quickly. That first trip to the gym is always the toughest. A person who's overweight or out of shape will find a million different excuses not to go. The second trip is a bit easier, but still difficult. But what happens after the third workout? That same person actually finds himself wanting to go to the gym. He's excited about going. Before he knows it, there's nothing that can keep him from going. The reason is that the inertia that he originally felt has been transformed into momentum. And momentum is the single most important factor necessary to taking effective and sustained action. When you say to God "Please give me courage," one of the first things he's going to do is give you the nudge you require to start moving when you're feeling at your most lethargic — physically, emotionally, or spiritually. He's going to give you that little push you need so badly to get off your butt![7]

And that's just the start. Once you've been given the gift of courage, it doesn't just end there. Your courage will grow. Like all the virtues, it's a "muscle." If used, it will increase in power and size. The more you exercise it, the more God will give you. It's possible to be born with a very timid nature, afraid of your own shadow, and then, through prayer, begin receiving "infusions" of courage from God. If that courage is nurtured and exercised, then it's possible for that same timid person to become, over time, the most heroic of saints.[8]

The problem is that this dynamic works in the opposite direction too. If a muscle is not used, it becomes atrophied — it shrinks. That's exactly what happens to courage when it's underutilized. There are people who go their whole lives without ever asking God for courage and without ever "practicing" to be brave in small things. Then when a real moral crisis comes along, a situation that requires the courage to take action that might be painful, sacrificial, and frightening, they fall apart. Sometimes these same people will complain about how hard life is and how especially difficult Christianity is, with all its demands, regulations, and commandments. The truth is that these folks just haven't "worked out" their courage muscle in a long time. They're in terrible shape, morally and spiritually. The famous Christian apologist G. K. Chesterton said it's not that the Christian religion has been "tried and found difficult," but rather that it's been "found difficult and left untried"!

Now, I don't mean to imply here that anytime you experience difficulty in changing your life, it means you're lacking in courage. There are plenty of people out there who are having a heck of a time overcoming their problems and yet are very brave by nature. But, unfortunately, inborn bravery isn't always enough. Take the example of people who are caught up in self-destructive addictions. These poor folks — who are often good human beings at heart — are literally trapped in the clutches of evil. Whether the problem is drugs, alcohol, gambling, or sex, trying to overcome an addiction is one of the most fearsome struggles a person can ever engage in.

Having an addiction drains you of your ability to think about anything else — including God. All your energy is sapped, all your momentum is lost, all your hope is gone. You become enslaved in the truest sense of the word. Breaking those shackles and escaping from that bondage is so incredibly difficult that it requires the greatest courage in the world. There's simply no way anyone can do it on their own. Often people try — with tragic results — for the end is usually the same: complete and utter ruin, sadness, despair, and eventually death.

Father John Corapi, who overcame a severe drug addiction before becoming a priest, compares the struggle to mortal combat on the battlefield. If your opponent were somehow able to administer a pill or a poison that made it impossible for you to even raise your hands in defense, what would that mean to the outcome of the fight? Obviously you wouldn't stand a chance. That is exactly the strategy the Devil uses when it comes to addictions. Once a person is "hooked" on anything — be it heroin, liquor, pornography, or horse racing — that person can no longer make any progress in the spiritual life; nor can he help anyone else. Essentially, he's been rendered impotent.

The same can be true of phobias of various kinds. Having one or more can paralyze you. That doesn't necessarily make you a coward. An irrational fear is just that — irrational. But knowing that it's irrational doesn't make it any easier to deal with. Conquering such fears takes a lot of guts. There's a long process involved, and unless you've got an inborn, iron constitution, it's going to be very tough to get through it all.

In these cases, what God will essentially do when you ask him for courage is take you by the hand and lead you through the process. There are steps involved. Aside from admitting you're scared, you have to come to the realization that many other people suffer from the same problem, and that you're not any less of a good, kind, or brave person because of it.[9] You have to understand that your value and worth as a human being isn't decreased one iota because of the phobia; that you don't deserve any less respect or any less love than anybody else.

Then you have to identify what it is you're afraid of — which isn't always so easy. For example, if you are afraid of flying, you have to figure out exactly what part of flying is so terrifying. Some people are afraid of heights. Some people have claustrophobia and don't even know it — they're really afraid of being in the narrow, closed-in cabin. For some it's a control issue; they just can't bring themselves to trust the pilots. Some people have overactive imaginations and aren't able to stop picturing horrible crash scenarios in their mind. Instead of thinking about the great time they're going to have when they reach their destination, they focus on the incredibly unlikely chance of being twisted and burned in a fiery wreck. For these people, it's not so much a fear of flying they need to overcome; they need to develop the mental discipline to control their thought patterns.

Beyond this, there's a realization that must always take place: a realization that the short-term pain of facing a particular fear — great though it may be — is nowhere as terrible as the long-term pain that results from being incapacitated by that fear. People suffering from agoraphobia — the fear of open places — understand the pain involved in leaving the safety and security of their home. But do they really understand the pain involved in not leaving their house? Do they really understand how much their fear is going to hold them back in life, as well as the effect it will have on others they love? Do they really understand how much pain is going to be caused by living imprisoned in a life smaller, narrower, and less fulfilling than it could otherwise have been? No matter what kind of phobia you're battling, one of the ingredients to success is gaining an insight into how great the cost will be, long term, if victory is not achieved. That's the kind of insight God wants to give you.

And he wants to give you something else too — perseverance. It takes time to overcome fear of any kind. There are bound to be setbacks along the way — techniques and treatments that don't work, embarrassing falls and humiliations. It's at those times when the natural human tendency is going to be toward discouragement and despair. But if you pray for courage, you'll never get to that point — you'll never lose hope. You'll receive all the bravery and strength you need to carry the cross you've been given — just as Christ, himself, carried his cross. Thomas Aquinas thought this was the highest form of courage: the ability to sacrifice yourself, to endure, to "bear up" against terrifying circumstances over a sustained period.

You see, in the end, it all comes down to sacrifice. We've talked about the various "methods" people use to overcome their fears, but when you get right to the crux of the matter — the core of courage, so to speak — you realize that the truly courageous person is the one who is ready to sacrifice himself and his desires for the sake of something greater. The reason he's able to do that is because he knows in his heart that everything belongs to the Lord. He knows he can never really "lose" anything — since he never really "owned" anything to begin with. So many of our fears in life are tied to the fear of loss, the unwillingness to part with people, places, things, and activities we feel we have a claim on. But when we truly believe that God has dominion over everything — even life itself — then something mystical takes place in our souls, and all our fears disappear.[10]

In the famous final scene from the movie *Casablanca,* Humphrey Bogart sends the beautiful Ingrid Bergman away with another man so that he can stay behind and fight the Nazis. "I've got a job to do," he tells her. "Where I'm going you can't follow. What I've got to do you can't be any part of." Bogart, who seems to be such a hard-hearted cynic on the outside, ends up sacrificing everything — the woman he loves, a prosperous nightclub, the respect and status he has acquired in Casablanca — all because he knows there is something more important in life: the need to fight evil.

Ultimately, that's why we need to pray for courage. All the things in life we want to hold onto — our possessions, pleasures, and feelings of security — as well as the fears we have about losing them, are secondary to our struggle with evil.[11] As we've seen, the evil can be on the outside, in the form of a great social injustice, a natural catastrophe, a building on fire, or a neighborhood bully; or it can be on the inside, in the form of a phobia, an addiction, or a crippling physical ailment. Whatever the particular evil happens to be, we have to be willing to relinquish all our fears in order to face it and, hopefully, conquer it.

The word "relinquishing" appears so much in spiritual literature. It has to do with "letting go of the wheel" so that God can take control of things. It has to do with emptying ourselves of all our insecurity and pride and ego and woundedness so that God can come in and fill us up with himself. "Less" of us and "more" of God is always the formula for success when it comes to dealing with our human frailty.[12] Saint Paul said in one of his letters, "My strength is made perfect in weakness."[13] The reason is that when we are weak, we're in the perfect position to receive abundant graces from God. It's when we are filled up — with pride in our own skills and natural abilities — that we have no room for God's gifts. But when we are "empty," there is plenty of space for God to work in. He can come in and literally pour his spirit and his power into us. He's free to fill us with the highest-octane fuel imaginable, so that we can rocket right through any fears we have.

The bottom line is that when you feel yourself becoming afraid of something, you shouldn't worry at all. In fact, you should rejoice! Whether you're trying to muster enough bravery to make a speech, get on an airplane, take an unpopular stand, defend the defenseless, or rid a house of demons — the fact that you're scared only means that you have more potential inside you to be heroic. For God truly is the "Lord of Hosts," which means he is the God of all "righteous and victorious fighting forces" and the source of all courage. With that courage — his courage — nothing will ever be able to stop you, not even death.

In the truest sense of the word, you'll be invincible.

8

SOMETIMES BEING
SMART JUST ISN'T
ENOUGH

GOD, GIVE ME WISDOM

It has been said that God has placed obvious limits on our intelligence — but none whatsoever on our stupidity. Certainly there have been times in my own life when I've found that to be the case!

In a way it's unfortunate that God has set things up in this manner, since we're living in an age when intelligence is so critically important to determining our fate. Think about the vast number of challenges we face in today's world. We've still got all the age-old problems to deal with — problems of the heart, problems of the spirit, problems of love and war and honor and duty. Those problems have always been with us and will continue right on to the end of time. But in addition to them, we've got a slew of other issues to contend with that our grandparents never even dreamed of. The technology explosion and computer revolution of the last century have radically changed the entire socioeconomic landscape. Today, it's not enough to figure out what you want to do for a living, whom you should marry, and where you're going to live; you also have to know the answers to questions like "How can I hold a full-time job and be a good mother at the same time?" "How can I get out of all my credit card debt?" "How can I keep my children from smoking, drinking, having sex, and trying drugs, when I know their friends are doing those things?" "How can I bond with my son when all he's interested in is video and computer games and online chatting with his friends?"

The list goes on and on. It would be wonderful if we could just push a button and get all the answers. But of course we can't. We have to go searching — we have to read books, listen to CDs, go to seminars, consult with experts. We have to educate ourselves about practically everything in life, because life has become so very complicated. But do you know the problem with this strategy? It doesn't always work! In fact, sometimes it can have the opposite effect.

Have you ever come across a college professor who's got twenty letters after his name and almost as many degrees and yet absolutely no common sense? Or a theologian who's written dozens of books and taught at the most prestigious religious universities and yet denies the most fundamental doctrines of faith? Or a psychologist who has spent decades studying Freud and Jung and Skinner and yet does more psychological damage to his patients than good? I'm not disparaging academics or theologians or psychologists; what I am saying is that it's sometimes possible to educate yourself right into a state of idiocy!

You see, the ability to "figure out" the right thing to do isn't always tied to "book smarts," and the ability to see the "truth" isn't necessarily related to the amount of knowledge you possess. Yes, it certainly helps to be "smart" in life. But being smart isn't always enough. You have to have wisdom, too.

Human beings have sought wisdom since time immemorial. Yet there's never really been a universally accepted definition for it. Most people would agree that being wise has something to do with a person's ability to make sensible judgments and decisions based on knowledge, common sense, and understanding. But it also involves the ability to look at a given situation from multiple angles and then discern the truth about it. Whatever the definition you're using, though, one thing is for certain: Wisdom is a rare commodity.

This is undoubtedly one of the reasons that young people have such a tough time growing up. In addition to all the emotional turmoil and uncertainty they have to face, they're also expected to make decisions that require the most profound wisdom — a wisdom that is usually far beyond their years, at least in terms of life experience.

Consider the question of which career path to choose. That's a momentous decision for a young person to have to make. The wrong choice could actually wreck one's whole life. If you have children in college, for example, what would you advise them to do? Certainly they could go see a guidance counselor at school. You could suggest that they could try reading books about different kinds of professions. You could give them the benefit of your own hard-earned wisdom.

But while all of these methods are helpful, none is really adequate. None of them is going to guarantee that they make the right choice. The reason is that no expert, no family member, no educational institution, and no book can possibly tell your children the future. None of them can accurately predict what's going to happen in the next two years, much less the next two decades.

Nor can anyone really know what's in another person's heart — what kind of work will give your children the greatest amount of joy and inner fulfillment. Even they don't know that yet. So while family and friends and experts can all help them, their advice is of limited value.

But there is someone out there who is not limited in any way. There is someone who knows exactly what's in your children's hearts and exactly what will make them happiest — because he created them. And that someone also happens to know the future — because he created and planned that too. Do you think it would help to consult with that someone when trying to make an intelligent choice about career paths? Do you think that someone might have one or two valuable things to say — things even the experts don't know?

God is in your children's future right now. He sees them as graying, elderly men and women, even at this moment. He knows how things are going to play out for them — which choices they'll make that will turn out to be right, which will be wrong, which will lead to good consequences, which to disasters. He sees their whole lives — from beginning to end — in one glance. Doesn't it make sense for them to ask God for some guidance? Not just on which career to choose, but on every matter of importance — including whom to marry, where to live, how to raise their children, how to figure a way out of debt.

And yet how many people do you know who actually consult with God on a regular basis? How many people pray to God for wisdom before making a major decision? Did you, for example, pray fervently before picking your major in college, or taking that all-important walk down the aisle, or buying your house, or deciding where to send your kids to school?

Human vision is so severely limited — both literally and metaphorically. Right now, for example, I'm looking at a model airplane that's on my desk. I can either look straight at the plane, or I can focus on what's in the background — on all the other things in my office. I can't do both. If I look at one, the rest is going to be blurry, and vice versa. That's true in life, too. When we attempt to "figure out" what to do in any given situation, we have a tendency to concentrate on either the short-term or the long-term results, on either our own self-interest or the good of those around us, on either the "big picture" or the details. We're always so busy trying to balance opposing points of view. The problem is that we can't do everything at once. Most times we fall short of the mark, because the equipment we're measuring with — our eyes and our minds — is limited to begin with.

Not so with God. His vision is all-encompassing. And this is really the best definition anyone can give you of wisdom. It's the ability to understand things from God's perspective, the ability to see things with God's eyes.

God, as we just said, is in the future; he knows how everything is going to turn out for you; he knows your big picture. But God also sees the intricate little details of your present-day life.[1] He sees everything that is happening to you now — all the ups and downs you're experiencing, every morning, noon, and night. Because he loves you and has your best interests at heart, he is intensely interested in those details and how they impact you, long term and short term. Indeed, Scripture says that "The very hairs of your head are all numbered."[2] Therefore, when you see with God's eyes, you're really seeing life from the widest possible perspective, but also from the vantage point that is most focused on you and your own personal happiness.

It's a great gift to be able to do that. It's

even more wonderful that God wants you to be able to do that on a regular basis. Wisdom is something God is ready and willing to give you. It's not some big secret. Saint James made that crystal clear when he wrote: "If anyone lacks in wisdom, let him ask God, who is always ready to give a bountiful supply to all."[3]

You see, God isn't only the source of wisdom — he is wisdom. In the Old Testament, we see God identified with wisdom on many occasions.[4] In the New Testament, we see that this is true of Jesus Christ in a special way. In the famous prologue to the Gospel of John, the evangelist calls Christ the "Word" and the "Light."[5] Both these terms signify wisdom. "Light" has to do with reason, understanding, and truth. "Word" has to do with the concept of self-expression. When human beings use words in conversation or in writing, they reveal who they are, what they're thinking, and what they're all about. The same is true of God. His "Word" is his own self-expression of who he is. And who he is — is Jesus Christ. Everything God is, says, teaches, desires, or thinks is summed up in the person of Christ.[6] This is important, because it means that wisdom isn't just some remote, elusive, and hard-to-understand concept. Wisdom is a person. And it's a lot easier to embrace a person than it is to embrace a cloudy abstraction.

When you ask God for wisdom, you are essentially asking him to give you the gift of himself. And as we've seen elsewhere in this book, that's something he's always eager to do. Remember, the goal of authentic spirituality is to be in union with God. That's what the whole spiritual life comes down to. When you're in union with God, you have direct and immediate access to all of the things that God is, and that includes peace, courage, love, wisdom, and truth. God wants you to have these things; he wants to shine his light on humanity, to speak his word unceasingly. Therefore he wants to pour out wisdom on all of us. This is not profound theological thinking, it's simple common sense.

Have you ever heard it said of anyone that they had "the wisdom of Solomon"? Solomon, according to Scripture, was the wisest man who ever lived.[7] There are several whole books of the Bible devoted to him. When King David died, Solomon became ruler of Israel. One night the Lord appeared to him in a dream and said, "Ask me for anything you want." Solomon thought hard about all the different obligations he had to fulfill as king and how overwhelmed he felt, and he decided to ask God for the wisdom of discernment so he could govern better. The Bible says that God was very pleased that Solomon prayed for this. He told him, "Since you have asked for wisdom and not for long life, or wealth, or the death of your enemies . . . I will grant your request and give you a wise and discerning heart."[8]

God was happy when Solomon asked for wisdom — and he's happy when we ask for it. God granted Solomon's request, and he'll grant ours, as well. The only question is, will this wisdom God dispenses actually help us to solve our problems? Will it be of any practical value? In other words, will the prayer *"Give me wisdom"* generate an answer to the kinds of questions we posed at the beginning of this chapter — questions such as "How can I juggle a full-time career and full-time motherhood at the same time?"

The answer is yes, absolutely — as long as we are careful to adopt the same kind of attitude toward wisdom that Solomon had. Solomon asked God to show him how to run his kingdom better, but he did so precisely because he wanted to serve God better. Behind his prayer for wisdom lay a great faith in the Lord and a desire to be in closer union with him. In the same way, when we wish to harness God's wisdom and utilize it in practical situations, we need to be sure that our ultimate goal is to serve God more effectively.

Let's say, for example, that you're struggling with debt. Obviously God can show you a way out of your financial mess. After all, he invented the planets and the stars — he can certainly figure out a way for you to pay your phone bill! If you ask him to give you a solution, he is going to lead you to the best answer, but the clarity and speed of his response is going to depend, in large part, on your attitude. What, exactly, is your reason for wanting to get out of debt? Is it just because you're tired of dealing with bill collectors? Is it because you want more money to spend on yourself? There's nothing wrong with these motivations. But if you're going to ask God for help, maybe you should try thinking along a different plane. If the anxiety you're experiencing as a result of your financial problems is affecting every area of your life in a negative way — including your spirituality — then perhaps getting out of debt will help you live a more godly life. If that's truly the case, then by all means, let God know! Pledge to him that you're committed to becoming a more holy person. I'm not saying you should make some sort of a deal with God. God doesn't "do" deals. But if you want God's help to get free of debt-related stress, the freedom you achieve needs to serve God's purpose, too. And his purpose is to make sure you live a life in closer union with him, so you can get to heaven. If you try to think in these terms when you pray for wisdom, instead of just lamenting your poor financial situation, you can be sure of a response from God.

Now, the solution he gives you might not be one you like — it might not be the easiest or the most painless in the world. It might involve going out and reading some good books on fiscal responsibility and investment strategy, and then implementing that strategy. It might involve making some donations to charities even though you need money yourself. It might involve sitting down with an expert and hammering out a realistic budget, and then sticking to it. It might even involve getting another job to supplement your income. And if you've already tried these things, it might involve trying them all again, this time with God's help and a little confidence! Who knows?

Whether you're trying to solve a financial problem, a family problem, or a work-related problem, the key, once again, is to keep praying that God will allow you to see with his eyes. God's eyes are all-powerful.[9] Not only can they see into the future, but they can see with perfect clarity. So often the reason that we have trouble deciding on the best course of action is that we're confused by all the details, variables, and circumstances that surround a particular problem. Added to that is the fact that we are often a jumble of conflicting emotions. It's not necessarily that we lack the will to act; it's just that it's easy for us to get stuck in a fog of confusion. Luckily, God's eyes are able to cut that fog. They see through all the extraneous, irrelevant, and distracting details. They see through all your own personal shortcomings, biases, and insecurities. They see through to the very heart of the matter, with a razor-sharp, diamond-clear clarity that will make it possible for you to finally understand what it is you're supposed to do.[10]

And with this new understanding will come something else, too: the mysterious ability to see a special kind of light, a light that originates in heaven and is only occasionally visible on earth; a light that has been glimpsed over the centuries by geniuses, artists, composers, and others fortunate enough to have been given the gift of creativity; a light known as inspiration. For when you see the world through God's eyes, you begin to see possibilities for solutions that would never have occurred to you under normal circumstances.[11] Ideas will suddenly pop into your head — great and wonderful ideas; life-changing ideas, ideas for books, businesses, and projects; ideas for the resolution of problems; ideas for advancing God's kingdom on earth.

Inspiration, clarity, focus, knowledge — all of these are the fruits of wisdom. Yet it's very important to understand that none of them is the same as *sanctity.* Indeed, one of the all-too-common side effects of these gifts is great pride. You can have the most inspiring insights in the world and yet do things that make God very angry. True wisdom, in contrast, always leads us to please God. Thomas à Kempis, who wrote the spiritual classic *The Imitation of Christ,* said: "What does it matter if you understand the profound mysteries of the Holy Trinity, and then displease the Trinity?"

I don't know about you, but I've fallen into this trap many times. It's easy to start feeling conceited spiritually after you memorize a few verses of the Bible, or write a particularly good paragraph on some doctrine of the faith. But lapsing into hypocritical behavior occasionally and then repenting of it is one thing; making it a way of life is quite another. I know one or two people who have a vast amount of theological knowledge and yet whose behavior is nasty, prideful, spiteful, selfish, and self-righteous on a regular basis. I wouldn't have thought it possible, but it is! These folks (and thank God there aren't many of them) are just like the Pharisees in the Gospels. They know everything about the letter of the law, but they violate its spirit every chance they get. They forget the most basic of biblical injunctions; namely, that "the fear of the Lord is the beginning of wisdom."[12] In the words of Jesus, they're like "white-washed tombs that are full of dead men's bones."[13]

So yes, it's important that you tread very carefully when you go in search of wisdom. In fact, you have to be especially cautious when you take up the study of theology. I've said this before, but theology isn't like other subjects. When you get a master's in science or literature or history or psychology, that degree verifies that you have attained a certain level of "mastery" over the subject. Not so with theology. You don't ever master that subject — it masters you! If you really, truly understand what theology is — the study of God Almighty — then it's impossible to ever gain superiority over it. Indeed, you must be humble, reverent, and obedient before it, just as you must be humble, reverent, and obedient before God himself. That's one of the reasons that Christ went out of his way to choose ordinary laborers to be his closest disciples.[14] He knew that it would be easier for tax collectors, fishermen, and repentant prostitutes to become holy than it would be for the intellectually elite.

But if you're somehow able to stave off spiritual pride, the wisdom you obtain as a result of this prayer will certainly give you many wonderful advantages in life. It will give you the power to see things as they really are; it will give you a deep understanding of the truth — about yourself, about other human beings, and about God; it will give you the ability to distinguish between good and evil, right and wrong, and the ability to act on that knowledge. Perhaps the greatest thing it will do for you, though, will be to provide you with a most amazing shortcut.

What do I mean by shortcut? It has been said that there are two ways human beings can acquire knowledge. One is to learn it through experience, study, and inquiry. The other is to "catch" it. When Albert Einstein was very old, he was asked by someone how he originally came to formulate his famous theories. He responded by saying that when he was a young man, he had seen a glimpse of a magnificent vision, a vision of sublime beauty — a vision of relativity — and that he had spent the rest of his life trying to describe and explain what he had seen in that one brief moment.

It's possible for wisdom to come to us just like that — in a flash, in a moment of light-filled grace. By opening ourselves up to the inspirations of God, and then following them wherever they lead us, it's possible to acquire a lifetime's worth of wisdom without actually having to live a lifetime.[15] In the process, we can avoid all kinds of terrible problems we might otherwise have been forced to confront. Consider a few simple examples.

There are many people out there who are filled with lust. Not for sex, but for something much more insidious — "status." These folks are willing to spend ten times as much money for an item than is necessary, all because they want to appear "rich," or "fashionable," or "in the know." Now, of course, it's not wrong to like nice things, or even to indulge in a little showmanship once in a while. It can be harmless fun — so long as you're aware of the truth. And the truth is that all status symbols, no matter how expensive and sought after, are illusory and therefore worthless. Unfortunately, many people go through their entire lives without ever learning this lesson. Then, at the last moment, when the curtain finally begins to fall, they come to the horrible realization that they've squandered all the precious time God has given them on the most frivolous of pursuits. Like Tolstoy's fictional character Ivan Illyich, they're forced to admit that they lived their whole life "the wrong way." Had these people prayed for wisdom at an early age, they would never have made such a fundamental mistake. Why? Because at the heart of Christianity is the message of humility and self-sacrifice — the very opposite of vanity.

Similarly, couples who have been together for many years will almost always tell you that the key to a happy marriage is compromise. You have to learn how to give and take, how to respect the other person, how to sacrifice your own desires for the sake of your spouse. They'll often tell you that it took them a long, long time to acquire this knowledge; that marriage was a great struggle for the first five years or so, and that they finally got tired of fighting with each other and started working together instead. This is great advice. The only thing is, you don't have to fight like cats and dogs to get there! It's right there in the Gospels and letters of Saint Paul. The meaning of marital love is to give yourself completely to your spouse, body and soul.[16] The purpose of marriage is to reflect the love God has for us in such a profound way that new life is brought forth. And how far does God's love extend? To the death. That's how great the love of a husband and wife has to be. Now, you can be sure that if young married couples prayed for wisdom together each night, they would no doubt come upon this fundamental insight before too long; and if they took it to heart and tried to put it into practice, they certainly wouldn't be fighting as much.

In the same way, you'll often hear elderly people say that "the most important thing in the world is health." They've likely experienced some health problems in their latter years and have come to realize that all the good things in life — money, possessions, vacations, and so forth — don't mean too much if you can't enjoy them. After all, if you have a bad heart, or a bum leg, or such severe arthritis that you can't even walk, what does it matter what your bank account looks like? And yet many of these same people spent years abusing their bodies by smoking, drinking, and overeating. Did they really have to come down with some crippling ailment in order to realize the overarching importance of health? Of course not! Have you ever heard the expression "Your body is the temple of the Holy Spirit"? It's right there in Scripture.[17] It's been there for thousands of years — way before all the current dieting and exercise fads. A temple is not just any building. It's a sacred, holy place — a place to be treated with the utmost honor and respect. If the body is a temple, then it's obvious that it should be nurtured, cared for, and treated the right way. You don't have to be sixty-five years old to understand that. And you don't have to be superintelligent to see how this teaching not only relates to the idea of losing a few pounds, but is tied into the whole question of health and physical well-being. You just have to have a little spiritual wisdom, and then the courage to act on it.

Finally, several years ago I attended the funeral of a young girl who had committed suicide. She had been addicted to drugs and suffered from some psychological problems. At the end of the night I went to say good-bye to the mother of the girl, and she grabbed me by the arm and told me with tears in her eyes, "Make sure you hug your children tonight! Please, tell them you love them! It's so important that you do that." Tragically, she hadn't told her own daughter that she loved her very often, and now she couldn't. She was trying to impart that sad piece of advice to me while I still had the chance to avoid her mistake.

Once again, did she really have to acquire that wisdom at such a late date and at such an immense cost? Had she been praying to God for wisdom right along, is there any doubt that she would have been given the grace to understand the value of open, loving communication? Is there any doubt that God, who encourages us to communicate with him all the time through prayer, would have inspired her to express her feelings of love for her daughter sooner?[18]

These are all basic points, I know. But they're so vitally important. I'm not saying that if you pray to God for enlightenment you're going to magically avoid hardship and suffering. Nothing can prevent that. Nor am I saying that it's a bad thing to acquire a certain amount of wisdom through experience. Indeed, part of the fun and adventure of life is making mistakes and then learning from them. But profiting from your errors is one thing; wasting whole decades in search of readily available truths is quite another.

It all comes down to a simple choice you have to make. How do you want to learn the important things in life? Do you really want to study at the school of hard knocks? Do you really want to spend your time continually reinventing the wheel? Do you really want to wait till you're old and gray and battered and broken before you finally start doing things the right way — God's way?

Remember the famous final lines of Robert Frost's poem "The Road Not Taken"?

Two roads diverged in a wood, and I —
I took the one less traveled by,
And that has made all the difference.

Praying to God for wisdom is like taking the road less traveled. Most people you meet in life choose to go down the wider, longer road of experience.[19] You don't have to!

You don't have to have your son or daughter die before you learn the importance of expressing your love; you don't have to contract some god-awful disease before you realize that wealth and popularity are vastly

218

overrated and that the most important thing in life is not love of self but, rather, love of God and neighbor.[20] You don't have to make a million mistakes or live to be a hundred to learn any of life's great lessons.

Wisdom doesn't have to be "wasted" on the old like youth is wasted on the young. It's available to everyone, free of charge. All you have to do is take the shortcut that God has provided. All you have to do is ask.

9
WILL I EVER BE HAPPY AGAIN?

GOD, BRING GOOD OUT OF THIS BAD SITUATION

"God, please bring some good out of this bad situation" is one of the most powerful prayers in the universe — and one that God always says yes to — but it's also one of the toughest to pray. The reason is that when we're right in the midst of suffering, it's very hard to calmly consider all the wonderful things that might lie in store for us in the future. After all, the future is always so unclear and hazy, while the pain we're experiencing in the present moment is so sharp and unmistakable. That's why clichés like "look at the bright side" and "every cloud has a silver lining" can be off-putting and even slightly nauseating when we hear them.

And yet expressions like these don't usually become clichés unless there is some truth to them. Somewhere along the line, human beings noticed that bad things can give way to good things or even *lead* to them. In fact, if it weren't for the bad experiences — the failures, the humiliations, the tragedies — sometimes the very best experiences in our lives would never have occurred. The entire personal development/ self-help industry is founded on this one point: the principle that nothing is truly bad unless we *think* it's bad; the view that there are no such things as "problems," only "challenges" and "opportunities for growth."

There are thousands — perhaps millions — of stories of people who have suffered through terrible ordeals and yet found the faith, strength, and courage to keep their heads up and eventually triumph over their tragedy. Personal development experts and motivational speakers often use these stories to help people persevere through their struggles; to give them hope that their failures and their tragedies aren't the end of the story, but only a new beginning.

One story about overcoming adversity that has always stood out in my mind concerns the great president Theodore Roosevelt. Because of his fame as a tough, courageous leader, not many people know that Roosevelt was also a very romantic man — at least when he was young. When he was in his early twenties he fell head over heels in love with a beautiful black-haired girl named Alice. He wooed her for two years before she finally consented to marry him. To say that he was hopelessly, passionately in love with her would be an understatement. She was, for him, the sun, the moon, and the stars; she was his everything. His diary entries about her at that time reflect a passion bordering on obsession and even worship. When she informed him that she was pregnant, his happiness became even more ecstatic.

Then the unthinkable occurred. The very night that Alice gave birth to their child, she was afflicted with a rare condition called Bright's disease, which immediately began attacking her kidneys. Roosevelt rushed to her bedside and tenderly cared for her. But at the exact moment this was happening, Roosevelt's mother — who lived in the same house — suddenly began to burn up with typhoid fever.

For the next sixteen hours, Roosevelt went back and forth between his mother, on one floor, and his wife, on another. They were both suffering terribly, and there was nothing the doctors could do for either of them. His mother was the first to die, in his arms, in the very early morning. Later in the afternoon of that same day his beloved Alice died as well, also in his arms. The date was February 14, Valentine's Day.

A few days later there was a double funeral, and a dazed Roosevelt, barely able to talk, wrote down the following epitaph for his wife: "We spent three years of happiness greater and more unalloyed than I have ever known fall to the lot of others. . . . For joy or for sorrow, my life has now been lived out." A little later he added: "She was beautiful in face and form and lovelier still in spirit. When she had just become a mother, when her life seemed to be just begun and the years seemed so bright before her, then by a strange and terrible fate death came to her. And when my heart's dearest died, the light went from my life forever." In his diary Roosevelt drew a thick black X on the page marked February 14 and repeated the words: "The light has gone out of my life forever."

Theodore Roosevelt was only twenty-six at the time. He was a completely broken man, emotionally and spiritually. He was numb, inconsolable, and in his heart and mind he was done with happiness, done with people, done with work, done with living. He truly thought that the light had gone from his life. And yet we know that just the opposite was true. Indeed, the glory and grandeur of his monumental life had not yet even begun to shine. In just a few short years, he was to become a war hero, an author, the winner of the Congressional Medal of Honor (awarded posthumously), the recipient of the Nobel Peace Prize, a famed outdoorsman and conservationist, a happily married father of six, and the man who, as twenty-sixth president of the United States, was ultimately responsible for making America a global power. All of these triumphs came *after* he had been dealt the most crippling blow of his life.

So yes, happiness and success can come after even the worst sorrows. But do they always? Unfortunately, the answer is no. For every inspirational story like Teddy Roosevelt's there seem to be dozens more with unhappy endings. So many people who go through great suffering become cynical and depressed, closing themselves off not only from other people but from the very possibility of experiencing joy again. As the saying goes, they live lives of "quiet desperation." Self-help experts would say it doesn't have to be that way, that such people have the ability within them to turn things around, if only they wanted to.

But these experts miss one all-important point: overcoming adversity is not just a question of willpower. It's not just a question of being motivated to "look at the bright side" or to "think positive." It's not even just a matter of focusing on the solution to your problems and taking action. All of those things may be important, but at its core the question of how to transform suffering into happiness is still a religious one. Ultimately, it is *God alone* who has the power to bring good out of bad.

Back in Chapter 4 we discussed the subject of human suffering and said that it was one of the greatest mysteries in all theology. We said that God always answers the prayer *"Please get me through this suffering,"* but that he doesn't always tell us what the purpose of that suffering is. Well, while it's true that God doesn't always reveal to us the reasons for the bad things that happen, he does do more than simply promise to "get us through." He also pledges, to those who ask him in prayer and to those who are trying their best to do his will, that he will bring good out of every single misfortune they encounter in life; that he will somehow, in the end, turn every instance of suffering into an opportunity for greater, deeper happiness.

If you were going to memorize only one verse in Scripture, Romans 8:28 might be the one to choose, because it holds the key to this promise. If you learn it — really, truly learn it — it will be the spiritual equivalent of having a protective coat of armor about you at all times. The "slings and arrows of life" may indeed knock you down and cause you injury, but none will ever penetrate so deeply that you will be overcome and destroyed. The verse simply states: *"All things work together for good, for those who love God and are called according to his purpose."*

All things work together for good. The Bible doesn't just say that *some* things will turn out to be good in the end. It says *all* things. In other words, if you are trying your best to be the kind of person God wants you to be, then everything you do, everything you fail to do, and everything that you experience in life — even the worst tragedies — will yield some kind of greater "good" in the end.

Now, how can that possibly be true? How can all things work for good? How can losing your job ever lead to good? How can having financial problems ever lead to good? How can being handicapped ever lead to good? How can getting cancer ever lead to good? How can any of these things lead to anything good, when we know that they make us feel so bad?

Perhaps the main thing to understand in

this discussion is that while it may be impossible for us to fully grasp *how* God can pull good out of every bad situation, he has already shown us that he *can* do it. He has already demonstrated to us that he has the ability, if he chooses, to pull the best kind of good out of the worst kind of evil. When, exactly, did he do that?

Think about the greatest evil ever to take place in the history of the world. No, it wasn't the Fall of man; it wasn't the killing of Abel; it wasn't any of the bloody events of the Old Testament; it wasn't the Spanish Inquisition or the Crusades; it wasn't the brutal regimes of the Nazis or the Communists; it wasn't the terrorist attacks of September 11; and it wasn't any of the personal tragedies that we experience in our own lives. No. The greatest evil ever committed was the *murder of God.* When Christ was executed on Good Friday, God himself — in his human form — was put to death. Here we have without question the greatest single act of disloyalty, ingratitude, deception, faithlessness, betrayal, depravity, obscenity, malevolence, and outright evil of all time. God — who created everything and everyone — was actually killed by his own creatures. The crime was not simply homicide or patricide or fratricide, it was *deicide.*

Truly it is impossible for there to be anything worse than that. No tragedy in life, no matter how appalling, no matter how disastrous, could ever come close to the Crucifixion and death of our Lord.

And yet what did God manage to do with this most monstrous of all human events? Did he allow our situation to stay lost and hopeless for long? Did he give up on mankind? Did he give up on all creation? Did he for one second concede that Satan and his demons had won the day? No. Instead, God promptly turned the world and everything in it on its head. For out of the hellish darkness of the Crucifixion he brought the miraculous light of the Resurrection. In one amazing stroke of genius and grace, God turned it all around — he redeemed mankind, elevated the human person to a divine level, made it possible for sins to be forgiven and for us to receive countless blessings during our earthly lifetime. On top of this he threw open the gates of heaven so that one day we could all be reunited with our friends and loved ones in an eternity of happiness.

Do you see what God did? He didn't just bring a little good out of a little evil. He didn't just bring a little good out of a lot of evil. Somehow, some way, God was able to bring the *greatest* good out of the *greatest* evil! No more horrible event could have taken place than the killing of Christ. No more wonderful treasure could have been given to mankind than the Resurrection of Christ. In rising from the dead, God didn't just "fix things up" or "make things better" for us. He did something much more profound. He turned black into white, dirt into gold, sin into eternal life.

There's a great lesson in this for us. For if God was able to turn the worst kind of evil into the greatest kind of good, then he can certainly turn *lesser* kinds of evils into good as well. He can certainly take the bad things that happen to us in our lives and bring some kind of blessing out of them. Doesn't that make sense?

Now, how he does that is not always so apparent. When you're struggling to pay your bills, or crying over a broken relationship, or sitting in a funeral home mourning the loss of someone you love, it's pretty hard to imagine how God could ever turn your sadness into joy. When you're in that kind of state, it's difficult enough not to be angry at God, much less have confidence in his power to give you happiness. And yet he can.

We said earlier in this book that God allows plenty of bad things to happen in life, but that he doesn't purposely cause them. He's not some sadistic monster who gets pleasure out of watching his creatures suffer. On the contrary, God mourns *with* us when we are in agony. He is just like any father who feels bad when his child falls and hurts himself.

Nevertheless, there's also no doubt that God is in complete control of everything that happens in the universe at all times. Even though he hates it when we suffer, he definitely permits many awful things to occur. He does so because he knows full well that he has the power to bring good out of them. He knows full well that his overall plan — which is always to our benefit — is going to be accomplished.

Now, I warn you, we are entering into the most mysterious area in all theology, and even the language we use is going to become suspect and confusing. It may appear at various points in the next few pages that I am trying to imply that God is responsible for *causing* pain in order to *force* human beings to act in certain ways. That is not the case. God is not a puppeteer, and we are not his marionettes. God is not a chess player, and we are not his pawns. At the very same time, though, it is one hundred percent accurate to say that "not a single sparrow falls to the ground without the permission of our heavenly Father." It is one hundred percent accurate to say that "every hair on our heads is numbered."[1] It is one hundred percent accurate to say that God "uses" the bad things he knows are going to happen in order to achieve the good things that he desires.

This great paradox — how God can remain "in charge" and yet allow mankind to have free will — lies at the very crux of the problem of human suffering. We frankly don't know how God is able to reconcile such seemingly opposed realities. The only thing we can say for sure is that it has something to do with the fact that he does not "exist" in the same way that human beings do. It has something to do with the concept of "time," and the fact that God has the ability to see the "big picture."

As I said in my book *A Travel Guide to Heaven,* human beings

> have a past, present and future. We experience life as a series of progressive moments, and can never know for sure what the next moment will bring. It's not like that for God. God stands outside of time. When he looks down from heaven at

John Smith's life, he doesn't just see John the way he is now. He sees all of John's life, from beginning to end. It's as if he's looking at a page titled *John.* He can look up at the top of the page and see John's birth, he can look at the middle of the page and see John getting married, and he can scroll all the way down to the bottom of the page and see John dying in the hospital with his grandchildren around him. He sees it all in one glance. God sees all the choices we're going to make in our lives, and all the results of those choices. He sees the mistakes, the sins, the screw-ups. He sees everything we're going to do, and he sees it all ahead of time. In order to accomplish his will he takes all these choices and *arranges* them in such a way that his plan is ultimately achieved.

Some way, somehow, God is able to *orchestrate* what freely happens on this planet, in order to produce the outcome that he desires — without taking away one iota from our freedom.

Oftentimes it's easy to recognize the sort of "outcomes" God is trying to produce. Suffering — even the worst kind — can have obvious benefits. It can, for example, help to make a person stronger, tougher, and more resilient — as in the case of Teddy Roosevelt. Those are qualities that come in pretty handy in life. Indeed, many who have gone through the furnace of human suffering credit their trials with helping them to become the men and women they are today. Enduring the so-called "refiner's fire" is what shaped and forged them — perhaps more so than any other experience.[2] Saint Paul said that "suffering produces endurance, endurance produces character, and character produces hope."[3] Hope is often the most important gift we can impart to each other. When you've suffered a great deal and yet managed to emerge with your strength and hope intact, you can be of tremendous assistance to others.[4]

Moreover, when you're experiencing pain, the people around you have the opportunity to be loving *toward you.* People who might otherwise be cold, selfish, and disengaged suddenly have the chance to become caring and compassionate human beings because of their relationship with you. Your suffering can therefore help them to become closer to God. It can be a doorway to grace — and even to heaven — for someone else.

As we discussed previously, suffering will usually make a person more dependent upon God and therefore more open to embracing his will. "There are no atheists in foxholes," as the saying goes. When you're in a weakened, vulnerable state, afraid for the future, afraid for your loved ones, afraid for yourself, you're more likely to be humble; you're more likely to give God the chance to come into your life and transform it. Augustine of Hippo put it beautifully when he said only those who have open arms and open hands are able to receive God's gifts.

Most Christians believe that suffering has a "redemptive" value. There's a mysterious line in Saint Paul that says: "In my own flesh I fill up what is lacking in the suffering of Christ for the sake of his body, the church."[5] Catholics have always interpreted that to mean that God gives us the ability to somehow "attach" our suffering to the Cross, and that all the pains we experience in life can be used by God to help build up the "body" of his church on earth and in heaven. That's why you'll sometimes hear Catholics telling each other to "offer up" their pain to God. Not all denominations within Christianity go as far as that, but all Christians *do* acknowledge that God is able to connect a mystical value to our suffering that we can't always see.

Perhaps the greatest good that can come

of suffering is that it has the potential to make a person more Christ-like.[6] Jesus went through every kind of human pain imaginable, and he did so because he knew that *we* would be going through plenty of pain as well. When you're hungry or hurt or poor, when you're in chronic physical pain or confronted with infidelity and disloyalty, when you're imprisoned or lonely or separated from your family for long periods of time, when you're persecuted because of your faith — when you go through any of these agonies, you're experiencing the very same things that God himself did. Therefore, it's possible to be even closer to him and more like him. This closeness and intimacy with the Lord can actually bring you a kind of joy and peace you cannot find anywhere else in the whole world, because it flows directly from being in union with God.[7]

Sometimes the good that results from your suffering becomes apparent only after the pain has ended. If you lose your job but wind up finding a better position a few months later, then being fired actually turned out to be a blessing for you. It might not have seemed that way at the time, but in reality it was. I know people who toiled away for years in jobs they hated, but never lost faith in God and never stopped praying that they would be delivered. Eventually they were; and now, when they look back on their life, they realize that all the waiting and frustration were actually beneficial to them. In some way, their time in the "wilderness" is what made it possible for them to find true happiness. One thing you learn as you progress in the spiritual life is that God is a God of *perfect timing.* Since he is able to see the "big picture," he knows just when you should move on and when you should stay where you are. And sometimes before you move on he has to "arrange" a thousand different details in order to make that move possible. That arranging takes time.

People who travel frequently on airplanes know just what I mean, because they have experienced the frustration of "circling." Usually this happens near the end of the flight, just when you're most anxious to get off the plane. Your seat belt is fastened, your tray table is up, and after hours of being cramped into the same tiny position, you're finally ready to come in for a landing. Then, for some inexplicable reason, the plane starts making a series of wide ninety-degree turns and it's apparent that you're not going to land after all. Instead, you've gone into the dreaded "holding pattern." You circle round and round, sometimes for a very long time, until air-traffic control finally clears you to descend to the airport. Sometimes the captain will come on the intercom and tell you the reason for the delay, but most times he won't, and you just have to sit there and wait. There might be a dozen other planes ahead of you that have to land or take off. There might be a thunderstorm in the vicinity of the airport. There might be a problem with one of the runways. Who knows? The point is that, despite the frustration of the passengers, and despite the pilot's ability to freely control his aircraft, another entity — air-traffic control — has made an overriding decision to prevent the plane from landing. And there's just nothing anyone can do about it.

The very same thing often happens to us in life. We can decide what we want to do and where we want to go, but God is still in charge of "air-traffic control." He sees everything on his omniscient radar screen — the weather, the airport, all the other planes in the area. Sometimes, for reasons he may or may not disclose, he decides that the best thing for us to do is remain in a "holding pattern." While we're busy circling, he's busy clearing obstacles, solving problems, and moving people around until

237

things are *just right.* Then and only then does he permit us to come in for a safe, smooth landing.

The amazing thing about this radar screen God uses is that it doesn't just show him the way things are at the present moment. It doesn't just depict the past, the present, and the future. It actually projects beyond the future and into eternity. We've already talked about how important God's perspective is in the pursuit of wisdom. Well, that's really the key to understanding this prayer as well. Because sometimes the only way to make sense of suffering is if we view it from the vantage point of eternity. Sometimes when a very bad tragedy occurs, it's impossible to see how God can bring good out of it. After all, how can something as awful and unthinkable as the death of a child ever lead to anything positive?

But what we must always try to remember is that God is primarily concerned about one thing: whether or not we make it to heaven. Next to that awesome question, everything else — even our suffering — means nothing.[8] As I've said elsewhere, if you die at ten years old in an automobile accident but go to heaven, then you had a successful life. If you die peacefully in your sleep at ninety, rich and powerful in the eyes of the world, but go to hell, then your life was a wasted tragedy. "What does it profit a man," Christ asked, "to gain the world but suffer the loss of his soul?"[9] We don't always see the truth of this, but God does. When we go to a funeral, or see someone in the street who is crippled or mentally retarded, we torture ourselves by asking all kinds of questions about how different or better that person's life could have been, or why God was so "unfair." But we rarely ask the one question that really counts: Is that person going to heaven? That's the only thing God cares about. That's the lens through which he views our lives.

And that's the lens we have to try to use, too. Even when someone we love dies and we can't understand why, we have to try to trust God and believe in our hearts that *God knows better than we do.* He knows everything about that person, and about what would have happened in the future to that person had he or she lived. And knowing all that, he also knows the best time to bring that person home to him.

Even in matters that don't involve death, God is always concerned, above all, with the state of our soul. If he sees that a person is headed in the wrong direction, he won't hesitate to use any means at his disposal —

including suffering — to get that person's attention and redirect him. To borrow another brilliant analogy from C. S. Lewis, "God whispers to us in our pleasures, speaks to us in our conscience, but shouts in our pains: It is His megaphone to rouse a deaf world."

More than anything else, pain gets our attention. It has the power to change our lives in ways that few other things can. It forces us to stop thinking about trivialities — trivialities that some people spend decades wasting their time on. It makes us think instead about ultimate questions of life and death, right and wrong, sin and forgiveness, mercy and obedience — questions that we should be thinking about *all the time.* In other words, pain forces us out of our own little world and propels us into a place where we'll be more likely to consider what is important to God. Ultimately, pain is one of the most effective tools God can use to mold us into the kind of creatures who can one day, hopefully, inhabit heaven.

Rev. John Corapi, whom I mentioned earlier, always urges his TV viewers to "be clay." What he means by that is that people need to be sufficiently flexible in their thinking in order to be able to listen to the will of God. After all, if God is an artist and one of his objectives is to make you into a better, holier person, then it matters very much what kind of "material" you're made of. If you're cold, hard, and inflexible, like marble, what would God have to do in order to change you? He certainly wouldn't be able to simply pull and stretch you gently into a different shape. That wouldn't be possible, because you'd be too unyielding. No, he'd have to take a mallet and chisel and begin hammering at you! He'd have to start knocking pieces of you to the ground. He'd have to literally cut chunks of marble out of you until you finally started to assume the shape he intended for you from the beginning.

Now, how do you think it feels to have pieces of yourself removed in this manner? Would it be a peaceful, gentle process? Would it be painless? On the other hand, what if you were made of clay? Then how would God go about fashioning you? To be clay, of course, means that you'd be softer, more easily modeled, more impressionable, more open to the creative desires of God — more open, in a word, to following God's will. The process of being shaped would be a good deal less dramatic, wouldn't it? A good deal less severe — and yes, less painful.

The bottom line is that God is going to do whatever he has to do in order to get you to heaven. If it requires using a hammer and chisel, he will. If it requires gently modeling and caressing you with his hands, he'll do that, too.

Let's use another example. Let's say you were in a deep sleep and just didn't want to get out of bed. You could be wakened in several different ways. The alarm clock near your head might go off, jolting you out of sleep. Someone might come along and yell in your ear or even physically shake you. Both methods would probably work. But there's another way, too. A less traumatic way. Someone in your family might go into your kitchen and quietly begin preparing breakfast. In your slumber, you might hear the eggs and bacon crackling on the stove. The delicious smell of coffee brewing might waft into your bedroom. Before you know it, you'd be opening your eyes yourself, without the need for an alarm clock ringing or anyone yelling in your ear.

Well, many of us are asleep and don't even know it. We're asleep to what really matters in life. And God knows that he needs to wake us up — soon — because life is so very short. Many times he tries the gentle approach first — the "breakfast" approach.

He gives us a million beautiful sights, sounds, and sensations to rouse us from our slumber. He gives us, first and foremost, the wondrous gift of life. He gives us the oceans and the mountains and the rivers and all the glories of nature to behold. He gives us the weather — gorgeous spring days, lovely winter snowstorms, and beautifully melancholy rain showers. He gives us an infinite variety of people to form relationships with — people with different gifts, different personalities, and different ways of adding joy to our lives. He gives us art and music. He gives us answered prayers. He gives us our families and our friends. He gives us love and sexuality. He gives us his church, with its prayers, songs, and liturgy. He gives us each countless personal blessings. *All* of these are simply the gentle proddings of God, and all of them are meant to wake us up so we can pay more attention to him and what he wishes us to do.[10]

But what happens when none of this works? What happens when, despite all the beauties and the blessings of life, we continue to go down the wrong path? What happens when we refuse to wake up to the importance of doing God's will, no matter how many times he gently tries to rouse us from unconsciousness? Sometimes — and this is awfully hard for us to admit — the only thing that makes us pay attention to God is pain. Sometimes the only thing that works is that blasted alarm clock!

I'm not suggesting here that if you were a godlier person, you would miraculously be protected from all forms of suffering. Obviously, that's not the case. Everyone has to face a certain amount of anguish in life. That's just a consequence of living in a fallen world. And it's very true that God sometimes allows his most saintly servants to undergo the greatest trials, because he knows that the experience will make them even holier — he knows it will make them even greater saints. That you will have to deal with your portion of suffering in life is a given; but why would you want to go out of your way to make the most painful kind an absolute necessity? You shouldn't force God into a corner and make it impossible for him to get you to heaven *except* through suffering. You should at least give him the option of taking you along a different route — of using a softer touch!

In other words, if you're going to suffer, let it at least be for a better reason than that you need a "wake-up call." Let it be because God wants to put you in a "holding pattern." Let it be because God wants to make you a stronger, more courageous person. Let it be because God wants you to carry your cross and imitate Christ. Let it be because God wants you to advance in holiness. Whatever the reason, don't let it be because you're hard as marble and God has no choice but to take a hammer to you. *Be clay!*

You see, God wants you to be happy — in this life and the next. He wants so much for you to be happy that he has even come up with a way of turning bad things into good. But, as with every other choice we have in life, he gives us the freedom to say no to him.

In a very crude sort of way, the choice we have about suffering is the same choice we have when it comes to throwing out the garbage. We can either put it in the recycle bin, or we can throw it in the regular trash can. God is the great, divine recycler of the universe. If we pray to him, *"Please bring good out of this bad situation,"* he can take any kind of pain we give him — even something as trivial as a toothache — and recycle it so that it actually benefits our soul in the long run. But, ultimately, it's *our* choice. If we like, we can simply dump all our suffering into the garbage can, and along with all the other waste products of society it will go straight into the landfill. Oh, the great garbage heap of wasted suffering in the world! How much refuse has accumulated there in the history of mankind? How many untold agonies have people endured without the slightest bit of good ever coming from them?

It doesn't have to be that way. Every one of your tears, every one of your weaknesses, every one of your humiliations, every one of your failures — every single bad thing that ever happens to you in life — can be *transformed.* Out of every adversity, God can produce some higher good. Out of every loss, God can find some marvelous gift to give you. Out of every death, God can bring forth new life — if only you ask him.

If you come away from this book with only one thing, let it be this: *"All things work together for good for those who love God and are called according to his purpose."*

10
WHY AM I HERE, ANYWAY?

GOD, LEAD ME TO MY DESTINY

Ernest Hemingway said that every person's life, truly told, would make a great novel. That sentiment applies perfectly to the final prayer we're going to discuss, *"God, lead me to my destiny."*

We hear it said all the time: "every one of us is special." We've been told this by our parents, by our teachers, by our pastors and priests at church, and by all those personal development gurus we see on television. But is it really true? Yes, everyone has a different set of fingerprints, different physical characteristics, different DNA, and so on, but does that really constitute being unique?

Years ago I was very cynical about spiritual clichés like this. Obviously there were certain people who were special — the billionaires, the geniuses, the heroes, the celebrities, the tyrants, the saints — all the people who somehow managed to stand out from the crowd. But what about the vast majority of human beings who lived and died in complete obscurity, many of whom were unsuccessful, unremarkable, unhappy, and unappreciated. Were they special, too?

As I came to understand Christianity better, I realized that they *were* special, because every human being has an extraordinary dignity simply because he or she is a child of God, made in God's image and likeness and redeemed by God's son.[1] I accepted the idea that human beings have a special kind of intrinsic value that transcends external appearances. I realized and understood that a homeless drug addict on the street might actually end up being a greater saint in heaven than the most powerful world leader. But even with that understanding, it was hard for me to believe that each and every human being was uniquely special *in this life.*

Ironically, it was science — not religion — that ultimately gave me a deeper understanding of human individuality. As I read more about biology and chemistry, certain "clues" about the uniqueness of the human person began to present themselves to me, leading me to an unmistakable conclusion. Indeed, when you really study the sciences — especially statistics — a great cosmic detective story begins to unfold, at the heart of which is the mystery of human destiny.

Did you ever think about all the factors that had to be in place for you to be born? About all the millions of tiny details that had to converge at just the right time and just the right place for you to come into this world?

Mother Angelica, the little Italian nun who founded Eternal Word Television Network, used to tell a story about her own mother as a very young woman. One day while she was washing clothes in the apartment where she lived, she started to sing. It wasn't something she often did while going about her chores. Something just came over her and she felt like singing. Just at the moment she began, a man driving along her street happened to hear her. He wasn't from the area and he wasn't going to any of the houses in the neighborhood. He was just passing through on his way to another section of the city. But he was so taken by the singing that he just had to stop his car and find the young lady with the pretty voice in order to compliment her. He did, and sure enough, they began dating. One thing led to another and they eventually married. The amazing thing is that if he hadn't decided to drive down that particular block at that particular time, and if she hadn't felt like singing at that particular moment, there would have been no marriage, no baby, no Mother Angelica, and no religious television network!

Everyone has a story like that. My own mother was sixteen years old when she met my father. One night her sister asked her to go dancing at the old Triangle Ballroom in Queens. My mother didn't want to go. She was tired. She didn't feel well. But her sister — my aunt Pauline — practically dragged her out of the house. Lucky for me that she did! Because the man who later became my father had also decided, at the last minute, to go to the same dance club. It's fascinating how such little "coincidences" can have such monumental consequences in our lives.

And yet are they really coincidences? Consider for a moment the incalculable odds you had to overcome when your parents came together in sexual union and conceived you.

In any single act of intercourse between a man and woman, approximately five hundred million sperm cells are deposited in the female. *Five hundred million!* And only one of those sperm cells is allowed entrance into the woman's ovum. At the moment of contact, when fertilization first occurs, a special chemical is released by the egg causing it to close off all other sperm. Every other sperm cell — having lost the great race for human life — dies.

Half a billion potential human beings, each one completely different from you, could have been born in place of you had not that one, unique sperm cell fertilized that one, unique ovum. In a very real sense, half a billion other potential human beings had to forgo life to make way for you. Half a billion other men and women, each with their own distinct physical traits — their own hair, eyes, and voices — and each with his or her own unique personality, never saw the light of day, so that you could live. We don't often think of it this way, but each one of us has already won a race in which we were five-hundred-million-to-one long shots.

In fact the odds were even greater than that. For not only did one particular sperm cell have to fertilize one particular egg in order to result in the person called you, but it all had to happen in an extremely short window of time. In any given month, there are only five or six days during which sexual intercourse can result in pregnancy. Had your parents not engaged in sex during that short fertile period — or had they practiced contraception — no child would have been

251

conceived.

In other words, if you were conceived on a Tuesday at ten p.m., that is the only time in all of history that *you* could have been conceived. A different instance of sexual intercourse at a different time would have yielded a different person because each sperm cell contains an entirely unique genetic code. The chances of the same sperm cell (the one that produced you) beating all those other cells on totally separate occasions are just infinitesimal.

When you throw into the equation miscarriages (one in five pregnancies), stillbirths (one in one hundred pregnancies), and abortions (one in four pregnancies), it's easy to see how stupendously lucky you were to be born at all. From a strictly statistical point of view, your presence on this planet is a miracle. At the very dawn of your life you had to overcome overwhelming odds — odds higher than any you will ever have to face in any other situation. No matter what you may think of yourself now, you are already an "overachiever" of the highest caliber. You have already proven yourself to be a kind of "superman" or "superwoman," conquering obstacles that were monumental in scope and proportion. No matter what ills may befall you in life, no matter what

252

suffering you may be forced to endure, no matter what family or money problems you may eventually have to face, it is imperative that you understand this: *You came into this world a champion.* Victory was your starting point.

And this is where we have to begin considering theology. Because the moment we start looking at God's role in the process of creation, we discover something very interesting. We discover that perhaps all of these amazing coincidences weren't really coincidences at all. We discover that there may be a very good reason why we were able to beat such formidable odds. There may have been someone who actually rigged the game at the start and fixed the odds for us. Indeed, throughout Scripture we see many mysterious references to the fact that God actually had knowledge of our existence *before* he created us.

For example, the Book of Jeremiah says: *"Before I formed you in the womb, I knew you, and before you were born, I consecrated you."* Psalm 139 says: *"Every one of my days was decreed before one of them came into being."* Saint Paul's Letter to the Ephesians says: *"He chose us in Him before the foundation of the world."²*

These verses all point to one thing: God

had us in mind even before we existed and even before the world was created. From the very beginning, he planned us. Therefore while it's true that we overcame great odds in order to be born, we did not accomplish this monumental task on our own. Our bodies and souls did not come about as a result of haphazard chance. They were engineered by an all-powerful God who wanted us — personally — to come into being. We may be statistical miracles, but we are not statistical accidents.

Think about what that means in practical terms. Before George Washington crossed the Delaware River, God already knew your name and date of birth. Before the Roman Empire fell, God already knew the color of your hair and eyes. Before the dinosaurs roamed the earth, God had already mapped out your entire genetic code. Before the big bang and the creation of the universe, God already knew that you would be reading this book now. Every hair on your head is numbered, says the Gospels — and was numbered before the very foundation of the world.[3]

There are some powerful implications that flow from all this. As we just discussed, God had to say no to a whole range of potential human beings in order for you to be born.

In that vast pool of potential genetic combinations, there may well have been individuals who would have turned out smarter than you, stronger than you, more beautiful than you. There may well have been individuals with personalities less prone to anger, greed, jealousy, and lust than you. And yet God said no to all of them.

Instead, God said yes to you. And in saying yes, he said yes to everything about you and the situation you were born into. He said yes to your looks, yes to your personality, yes to your particular gifts and skills, yes to your weaknesses. At the beginning of your life God gave his stamp of approval to every single thing about you. In his all-knowing providence he permitted a myriad of genetic and environmental components to come together to form you. Beyond that, he created your utterly unique soul out of nothing.[4] There's no getting around this fact: you have been specially designated and handpicked by God — chosen, in fact, over millions of other possible individuals — to take part in the life of this world.

The question is, why? What can it all mean? Why did God create us? And why did he make each of us in such a radically special way?

Common sense tells us that God must

have something in mind for us — something very specific. What else would account for his desire to make us so different from one another? Yes, it's true that God doesn't need anyone or anything, and that the main reason he created human beings was that he wanted to share his life and his happiness with us. But that still doesn't explain why he chose *you* to be born; why he chose *me* to be born. We're just too unique. A carpenter may enjoy fashioning wood into all sorts of objects, but when he builds something very particular like a chair or a table or a musical instrument, we have to assume he has some other purpose in mind for it, aside from simply satisfying his love of woodworking.

And therein lies the solution to the mystery, the key to understanding the whole enigma of human individuality. As we've said so often, we live in a broken, fallen world — a world that is badly in need of fixing. Despite all the beauty and goodness that surround us, there is no doubt that the world is filled with violence, unhappiness, confusion, depression, and death. God knows that the environment in which we live is drenched in suffering, and he has given us the privilege and honor of helping him alleviate some of it. Jesus Christ, the master carpenter, has chosen us to be his instruments to fix some part of this broken world.[5]

Each of us is special and unique because there is a special, unique mission for each of us to accomplish. Each one of us was chosen to live instead of countless other potential individuals because there is some objective that *only we* can accomplish. The reason why our lives have been so full of inexplicable twists and turns is that we were being specially prepared for this challenge. Despite all our character defects and weaknesses, we are the *perfect* individuals to tackle some specific problem in the universe that needs to be solved at this particular moment in history.[6]

In the final analysis, we are not just human beings but *keys* — keys that God has individually crafted to fit certain locks. Each of us is special because the lock we are called to open will accept only one key — one that looks different, acts different, and feels different from any other one; one that has different kinds of emotions, passions, skills, and defects from any other one. In fact, in all the world and in all of time itself, there has only been one key that has the ability to open this one particular lock — and *you* are it.

Make no mistake: when you find the lock, you will find your destiny. It could be virtually anything. It could be something big or something small, something loud or something quiet. It could be something that makes you famous overnight or something that keeps you hidden. It could be that you're destined to save someone's life in a fire or some other disaster — or that you're destined to change someone's life through a simple conversation. It could be that you'll one day create something that helps people — like an invention or a piece of inspiring music or a book or an article. It could be that your son or daughter is destined to achieve something stupendous — something he or she could never have achieved without your influence. Your destiny might be one decisive, dramatic moment in your life, or it might be many actions taken over many years. Who knows? Whatever it turns out to be, though, one thing is certain: it will be profoundly important to the life of this world and immensely fulfilling to you personally.

But there is one critical point to keep in mind: the destiny we're talking about here is not necessarily the same thing as your "dream." People always talk about how important it is to "follow your dream." And they're right — up to a point. I've had hundreds of dreams in my life: dreams of being a major-league ballplayer, dreams of being a doctor, dreams of holding elective office. At various times in my life I prayed very hard for these dreams to come true. But none of them ever did. Thank God! You see, no matter how much I might have prayed for those dreams to become reality, none of them was my destiny; none of them was what God wanted for me.[7] And none of them would have fulfilled me in the same way that I'm being fulfilled right now.

The fact of the matter is that no matter how much you love and cling to your dream, it may not be the reason you were created. It may not be the reason you were able to overcome all those astronomical odds and enter the life of this world. It may not be the purpose that God had you in mind to fulfill from all eternity.

Here's an example of what I mean. For the longest time my wife wanted to be a lawyer. Ever since she was a little girl, she fantasized about trials and juries and court-room dramas. In fact, when she was growing up she loved two things in life above all else: her dream of becoming a lawyer — and her father. She was extremely close to her dad. The two of them were practically inseparable. Of course, she loved her mom and brother and everyone else in her family, but she was definitely "daddy's little girl." Once when she was five or six years old, she overheard her father saying that he had to go out of town on a business trip. She suddenly got very worried. She went to her room and got her Snoopy electric toothbrush, her "feetie" pajamas, and a pair of socks and packed them all into her little round patchwork suitcase; then she put on her hat and coat and sat on the porch of her house waiting for her father to come out. When he opened the door and saw her on the steps with her quilted suitcase between her knees, he naturally asked her what in the world she was doing. She just said, "Daddy, I *have to* go with you — otherwise who is going to take care of you?" That's the kind of close bond they always shared. And they continued to grow closer as time went on.

Her dream of becoming a lawyer continued to grow as well. When she was a teenager, she studied hard, won various academic awards, and became a pre-law major in college. Then, as often happens in life, her plans got derailed. There was a death in the family that shook her pretty badly, and she decided to take a year off before going on to law school. During that time, she got a job as a kindergarten teacher. It was only meant to be a temporary position, a way for her to take a breather from life and save some money to help pay for law school.

But in that year something interesting happened. She realized that she *loved* her new job. She loved working with children and she loved watching them learn. She loved everything about being a teacher — from helping the kids tie their shoes and button their coats, to wiping their tears and blowing their noses, to teaching them the alphabet and getting them started on reading. Before she knew it, one year had turned into two, two into three, three into four. Her "temporary" job had become the passion of her life. All her past dreams of standing in front of packed courtrooms, delivering rousing closing arguments, and winning unwinnable cases completely evaporated. In the place of these fantasies were the real-life faces of little boys and girls who looked up to her with innocent, adoring eyes — almost as if she were a second mother. Even though she was making less money than she could have as a lawyer and her job was less "prestigious," she knew that what she was doing in her classroom every day was more deeply fulfilling to her than any dream could ever be. In short, she realized that she was living her destiny.

It would be enough if that were the end of the story. But it's not. God always has something else up his sleeve. About ten years after my wife became a teacher, her father was diagnosed with Alzheimer's disease. Anyone who has ever had a loved one suffer from this illness knows how horrendous it is. Not only do you forget people and places and memories, but you forget how to do the most basic things. You forget what knives and forks and spoons are for. You forget what numbers and letters look like. You forget how to button your shirt and tie your shoes. The burden is great for the people around you — especially your family. My wife's mother did a heroic job as the primary caregiver for her husband. But she couldn't do it all alone. She needed help. My wife, who was devastated by what was happening to her father, stepped up to the plate and did her part and much more. She went over to the house every day after school to help out. She took her father on weekend trips. She watched football games with him on Sunday. She spent every free hour she could with him. It was heartbreaking for her, but it was also very beautiful. She knew she was giving him a great gift.

She was returning a portion of the immense love he had showered on her throughout her life. Though she hated the disease with every inch of her being, she was grateful to God for giving her the ability to alleviate some of her father's pain and help him to maintain his dignity.

Then one day, not long ago, as she was zipping up his jacket, she had a moment of epiphany. Everything she was doing for her father — from tying his shoelaces, to showing him the difference between colors and numbers, to answering the same questions over and over again, to teaching him how to write his name — all of these things she had mastered as a kindergarten teacher. It was as if she had spent the last decade of her life being specially trained just so she could help take care of the one person she loved most in the world. She finally understood why it was that she had never felt compelled to complete her law studies — why it was that Providence had led her in a completely different direction. If she had become a lawyer as she had always dreamed, not only would she have missed out on helping all those little children, but she never would have been able to help her father in such a meaningful way.

Was it all just a coincidence? I don't think

so. The story is just too sublime. It's too full of love and self-sacrifice. It's too much about giving instead of receiving. It's too much about taking someone else's suffering upon yourself and transforming it into something that has lasting value. In other words, it has God's handwriting all over it.

So often the dreams we have are all about us and our desires and insecurities and vanities. They don't take God's wishes into the slightest account. Everyone has heard stories about unhappy movie stars, drug-addicted rock stars, disgraced public officials, and suicidal authors. All these folks achieved their dreams and yet they all came to the same unfortunate end. Why? One of the reasons is probably that their dreams did not coincide with their real purpose. They wanted something so badly — maybe it was fame, maybe it was riches, maybe it was power — but they failed to consider that perhaps this was the *last* thing they really needed, the last thing God had destined them for. Instead of trying to ascertain God's will through prayer and discernment, they essentially "forced" their key into a lock it was never meant for; they twisted it, struggled with it, pushed and jammed it — until it finally broke off.

There's no need for that ever to happen

to us. God knows the deepest desires of our hearts. He knows what will give us the greatest pleasure and the most profound happiness. Remember, he's the one who created us — he's the one who crafted the key — so he knows best what kind of lock it will fit into.[8]

The movie *Forrest Gump* is all about destiny. The main character, Forrest, is a simpleton; he admits that he's "not a smart man." But he "knows what love means." He spends his life trying to be a good, generous, and kind person — one who is open to embracing whatever destiny God has in store for him. "Life is a box of chocolates," he always says, and "you never know what you're going to get." He doesn't fight against the different kinds of "chocolates" he gets in life. He loves them all and "can eat thousands." This isn't so true of the people around him. The girl he's in love with, his lieutenant friend in Vietnam, and the various characters he meets in his travels — all are overly concerned with themselves and their problems. They desperately want to make their dreams come true. They want to create a destiny for themselves that *they* have planned. Though they're not bad people in any sense of the word, they're blind to the fact that God has a purpose in mind for them, a destiny that is much more glorious and grand than anything they might have imagined for themselves. But they don't want to consider that.

Instead, they try hard to fight their true destiny — and they suffer as a result. Not because God wants to punish them, but because their own nature and purpose for living are at odds with the false reality they're trying to create. Forrest's girl, Jenny, ends up becoming a lost soul who eventually gets AIDS. Forrest's friend Lieutenant Dan — who wants so badly to be a martyred soldier — loses his legs in the war and ends up becoming a cynical, belligerent invalid. Only Forrest, who is completely open to the will of Providence, achieves his true destiny.*

And it is a marvelous destiny indeed. Without even trying, he has the most adventurous and exciting life anyone could ever hope for: somehow he becomes part of all the historic events of his day; he receives awards, fame, accolades, the Congressional Medal of Honor, and billions of dollars besides. Why? Not because he's clever or handsome or talented or sophisticated or

* Jenny and Lieutenant Dan are finally redeemed at the end of the movie — because of Forrest.

charming or superior. But rather because he is open to the destiny that was meant for him; because he is willing to focus his attention on what really counts in life: being an honest, selfless, kind, obedient, humble, and godly human being.

Is the moral of this story that a person shouldn't try to pursue his dream and attempt to make plans for the future? Of course not. It's very important to do these things, but you must always keep in mind the words of the psalmist: "If the Lord does not build the house, its builders labor in vain."[9] As you dream and hope and plan and schedule, you must always remember that God already has something in mind for you — something that he's planned since before the world was created.

How do you find out what that "something" is? Ask him.

If you want to know your destiny, all you have to do is bring your request to God in prayer. After all, why would God want to keep something like that a secret from you if he's been planning it for so long? Of course he wants you to know your purpose in life, if only because he wants you to *get going* on whatever it is you're destined to accomplish; if only because he wants you to start fixing the problem in the universe that needs to be fixed.

That doesn't mean he's going to drop a letter into your lap that says: "Your destiny is X." This prayer isn't like some of the others in this book. It's not about instant gratification. It's more of a process. God is going to *lead you* to your destiny. He will point you in the right direction and spur you on, step by step.[10]

This prayer requires a little more patience than the other nine in this book. It requires the faith to trust God and the willingness to go down various roads you might be unfamiliar with.[11] In fact, saying this prayer is sort of like installing a divine GPS system in your car. The instructions you're going to get are progressive: "turn right here, turn left there, go forward now, stop for a moment, make a U-turn, and so forth."[12] Eventually, if you follow the directions — in other words, if you follow the promptings of the Holy Spirit — you're going to get to your destination.

There's a reason that God doesn't always tell us our destiny right away but prefers instead to reveal it to us little by little. It's because he's interested in not only what we're going to accomplish but also what kind of *person* we're going to be at the time we accomplish it. And sometimes the "journey" is what helps mold us into better human beings. Indeed, the journey is often what makes life enjoyable. All of the things we experience in life — from the time we're little children right up to the present moment — can help prepare us for the greatness God has in store for us. Even the bad things — the mistakes, the frustrations, the disasters and tragedies — can help lead us to our destiny. God wastes nothing. That's why we have to ultimately thank him for everything.[13] We have to ultimately say, in the words of one popular country song, "God bless the broken road that led me straight to you."

Of course, there may be a way to speed up the process. There may be a way to have your destiny revealed to you much more quickly than normal. If you're *already* the kind of person God wants you to be, then you might not need a long, hard, arduous journey to shape you. This is an idea we've come back to again and again. Whether you're trying to have a stronger faith, be more courageous, have the wisdom to know what to do, obtain peace in your life, or find your true destiny, it always helps to be *right with God.*

Getting right with God is the great shortcut, cure-all, and equalizer in life. It won't necessarily prevent you from suffering, but it will guarantee that you'll see God's plan for your life so much more clearly. And it will guarantee that you accomplish your role in that plan in the most effective, efficient way possible. I've known young people who were so solid in their faith that they were decades ahead of the adults around them in terms of their spiritual wisdom, maturity, and power of judgment. If they weren't living their destiny already, it was obvious that they were marching to it at breakneck pace. And then I've known men in their sixties — worldly men, well-educated men — who were completely lost. They didn't know where they were going, what their purpose was, or why their life mattered at all. I'm not just talking about men who were going through a routine midlife crisis. I'm talking about men who were fundamentally immature when it came to spiritual matters, lost souls with no conception of the fact that they had an incredible destiny they were called to fulfill.

So how does a person get right with God? By doing all the things we've talked about in this book: by trusting in the Lord and having faith in him. By trying to be obedient to his commands. By repenting when you fall. By having a spirit of thankfulness for all the blessings you've received — especially the gift of life. By being prayerful instead of prideful, humble instead of arrogant. By dedicating your life to serving others, just as God took on a human form so that he could serve us. In short, by being *in union* with God.

When you're in union with God, you're on the fast track to achieving your destiny. It doesn't matter how old you are, how young you are, how sick you are, how poor you are, or how limited you are. As long as you're alive, you have the power to accomplish the amazing things God has in mind for you. The problem is that there are a lot of people out there who have died on the inside even though they're still breathing on the outside. Do you know how you can tell if you've died on the inside? When you've given up on being a hero — when you've stopped believing that your life is every bit as great as a great movie or novel.

Never, ever do that! God certainly doesn't. It's impossible to overestimate this point. You can be going through tremendous suffering — you can be lonely and depressed and hurting in every way — and yet still perform great deeds. Always remember, we worship a suffering Lord. Therefore it's when you're suffering that you're *most* in union with God.[14] You're in the "power seat," as one preacher has said. The older you are and the sicker you are, the more potential you have to be a warrior for God. The more crosses you bear on your shoulder, the more ability you have to achieve true heroism in life. For when you're suffering as Christ did on Calvary, and yet have the faith and trust to say to God, *"Please lead me to my destiny,"* there's no telling what incredible miracles God will work for you and for those around you.

This isn't religious propaganda, it isn't the "power of positive thinking," and it's not a motivational speech. This is the truth. This is what faith in God is all about. Christ said, "Behold, I make all things new."[15] And that includes people's lives — at every stage. If you pray each day to God to lead you to your destiny, I promise you that death will not come before you have achieved it.

Do you know what the result will be? Your life will be a spectacular adventure. It will be faith filled, fun filled, and profoundly important. It will be a life of heroic service to everyone around you. It will be marked by extraordinary bravery and wisdom — and by an abundance of love, both given and received. Will there be suffering? Of course — as there is for everyone — but you will get through it all, with your faith and your peace of mind intact. In fact, your whole life will be one of peace — deep, abiding peace. And at the very end, when the time comes for you to leave this world, there will be no cause for regret. No tears because of a life misspent. No tragic sadness over "what might have been." You'll be able to rest easy in the knowledge that you gave God the honor that was due him and fulfilled the destiny for which you were created from all eternity.

And even then — even after you've finally breathed your last and your heart has stopped beating — even then, the great adventure will not be over. Because when you open your eyes again, the One who gave you life and gave the world life will look at you and say the words that all good people of faith everywhere yearn to hear, words that will give you a happiness far beyond anything you've ever experienced on earth: *"Well done, good and faithful servant . . . enter into the joy of your Lord."*[16]

THE "YES" PRAYER

With praise for all you are, Lord
And thanks for all you bless;
Lord, grant these ten petitions
With your eternal Yes:

Please show me that you're there
When I can't see your face;
Send troubled souls my way
Their wounds I will erase.

Let me see with your eyes
My mind with your thoughts fill;
But more than wisdom give me
The strength to do your will.

Bless me with abundance
Then put me to the test;
Gladly will I give you
Much more than I possess.

Send me your tranquility

In troubled times and calm;
With loving arms sustain me
Through suffering and harm.

Forgive me for my sins
Though legion they may be;
When death and evil triumph,
Bring good from tragedy.

But most of all reveal
The meaning of my life
The purpose of my glories
The reasons for my strife
My destiny in Heaven
No tears to flow again
My God please grant me all;
In Christ Our Lord,
Amen.

SCRIPTURE REFERENCES

Introduction: Too Good to Be True?
1. Romans 11:33.
2. Matthew 7:7; Luke 11:9.
3. Deuteronomy 30:19; Joshua 24:15; John 7:17; James 4:4.
4. Romans 8:28–29.
5. 1 John 5:14–15.
6. 1 John 5:14–15.

1. I Wish I Could Believe: God, Show Me That You Exist
1. Matthew 10:29–31.
2. Hebrews 1:1–3.
3. Genesis 1.
4 Genesis 6:18; 9:8–17; 12:1–3; 17:1; Exodus 20, 24; 2 Samuel 7.
5. 1 Kings 17; 2 Kings 2; 2 Kings 19, 20; Isaiah 1.
6. John 1:1–18; 1 John 1:1–3; Acts 2:1–4; 2:38–39.
7. John 15:15.

8. Luke 12:48.
9. John 20:27–29.
10. Acts 9:15–16; 26:20–21.
11. Matthew 4:5–7; Deuteronomy 6:16; Psalm 78:18, 41, 56; Psalm 95:9; Psalm 106:14.
12. 1 Timothy 2:3–4; 2 Peter 3:9.
13. James 4:8.
14. Revelation 3:20.

2. Why Should I Get Involved? God, Make Me an Instrument
1. John 15:13.
2. Matthew 26:26; Mark 14:22; Luke 22:19; 1 Corinthians 11:24.
3. Matthew 18:20.
4. Luke 1:26–45.
5. Luke 1:56.
6. Matthew 10:39; 16:25; Mark 8:35; Luke 9:24; 17:33; John 12:24–25.

3. What's in It for Me? God, Outdo Me in Generosity
1. Matthew 6:33; Luke 12:31.
2. Acts 4:13.
3. Isaiah 55:8–9; Romans 11:33.
4. Matthew 19:24; Mark 10:25; Luke 18:25.
5. 1 Timothy 6:10.
6. Matthew 6:19–20.
7. Isaiah 14:12–15.

8. Jeremiah 9:23–24.

9. James 2:1–5.

10. Luke 8:11–15.

11. Ephesians 5:5.

12. 1 John 2:15–17.

13. Matthew 27:57; Mark 15:43; Luke 23:51; John 19:38.

14. 1 Timothy 6:9; James 5:1–4.

15. Malachi 3:8–10.

16. Proverbs 19:17.

17. Luke 6:38.

18. Matthew 10:42.

19. Psalm 41:1–3.

20. Matthew 6:1–4.

21. Mark 12:41–44; Luke 21:1–4.

22. 2 Corinthians 8:12.

23. 2 Corinthians 8:1–4.

24. 1 Timothy 5:8.

25. James 2:15–17.

26. Proverbs 3:9–10; Proverbs 11:24–25; Proverbs 22:9; Psalm 37:25–26.

27. 2 Corinthians 9:6–8.

28. Psalm 50:10.

4. I Can't Take It Anymore! God, Get Me Through This Suffering

1. Matthew 26:36; Mark 14:32; Luke 22:39.

2. 1 Corinthians 10:13.

3. Luke 24:33.

4. Genesis 2:17; 3:6.

5. Genesis 2, 3.

6. Romans 5:12.

7. Genesis 3:8–10.

8. John 8:31–36; 2 Corinthians 3:17; Galatians 5:1.

9. Galatians 6:7–8.

10. Philippians 2:6–9.

11. Mark 15:34; Psalm 22:1.

12. Hebrews 4:14–16.

13. John 19:24.

14. 1 Peter 2:21–23; Isaiah 53:9.

15. Philippians 3:7–11.

16. Isaiah 43:1–2.

17. 1 Peter 1:3; Hebrews 6:19; Colossians 1:27; Romans 8:28–29; Romans 15:13.

5. Am I a Terrible Person? God, Forgive Me

1. Romans 5:8; Ephesians 1:7; 1 Peter 3:18; 1 John 1:9.

2. Romans 3:21–26.

3. John 19:28–30.

4. Genesis 3.

5. 1 Peter 4:6; Hebrews 11.

6. Romans 4:23–25.

7. Matthew 27:50–54.

8. Matthew 11:28–30.

9. Exodus 20; Matthew 22:39; Matthew 18:21–22.

10. 1 John 1:9.

11. Isaiah 30:18–19.
12. Ephesians 4:32; Colossians 3:13.
13. Isaiah 61:8; Hebrews 1:8–9.
14. 2 Chronicles 7:14; Jeremiah 31:34; Jeremiah 33:8; Jeremiah 36:3; 1 John 1:9.
15. Genesis 3:8; Numbers 32:23.
16. Romans 3:9–20; Psalms 5:9; 10:7; 14:1–3; 36:1; 53:1–3; 140:3; Ecclesiastes 7:20; Isaiah 59:7–8.
17. Mark 7:20–23.
18. 1 John 1:8.
19. Psalm 32:1–5.
20. 2 Corinthians 6:1–11.
21. 2 Corinthians 5:17–19.
22. 1 John 2:1–2.
23. John 8:10–11.

6. This Stress Is Killing Me! God, Give Me Peace

1. Proverbs 17:1.
2. Judges 6:24.
3. Isaiah 26:3.
4. Psalm 4:8.
5. Genesis 1.
6. Isaiah 54:11–15; Psalm 29:11; Psalm 85:8.
7. John 14:26–27.
8. John 20:6–7.
9. Isaiah 32:17; Isaiah 48:17–18; Romans 14:17; 1 Thessalonians 5:23–24; James

3:17–18.

10. Isaiah 48:22; 57:21.

11. Romans 5:1; Romans 8:5–9; Romans 14:17–19; Romans 15:13; Galatians 5:22–23.

12. Ezekiel 13:8–16.

13. Jeremiah 1:9–10.

14. Matthew 10:34–39.

15. Ephesians 2:11–18; Hebrews 12:14.

16. John 14:1.

17. Philippians 4:6.

18. Romans 5:1.

19. John 6:16–19.

20. Matthew 14:23–33.

21. John 16:33.

22. 1 Peter 5:7.

23. Philippians 4:6–9.

24. Colossians 1:15–20; John 20:19–23.

25. Isaiah 53:5; Numbers 6:22–26; 2 Thessalonians 3:16; Hebrews 13:20–21.

7. Okay, I Admit It: I'm Afraid: God, Give Me Courage

1. Genesis 15:1; 21:17; 26:24; 35:17; 43:23; 46:3; 50:19, 21; Exodus 14:13; 20:20; Leviticus 26:6; Numbers 14:9; 21:34; Deuteronomy 1:17, 21, 29; 3:2, 22; 7:18; 18:22; 20:1, 3; 31:6, 8; Joshua 8:1; 10:8, 25; 11:6; Judges 6:23; Ruth 3:11; 1 Samuel 12:20; 22:23; 23:17; 28:13; 2 Samuel

9:7; 1 Kings 17:13; 2 Kings 1:15; 6:16; 19:6; 25:24; 1 Chronicles 22:13; 28:20; 2 Chronicles 20:15, 17; 32:7; Nehemiah 4:14; Job 5:21, 22; 11:15, 19; Psalms 3:6; 23:4; 27:1, 3; 34:4; 46:2; 49:5; 56:3, 4, 11; 91:5; 112:7, 8; 118:6; Proverbs 1:33; 3:24, 25; 31:21; Isaiah 7:4; 8:12; 10:24; 12:2; 35:4; 37:6; 40:9; 41:10, 13, 14; 43:1, 5; 44:2, 8; 51:7; 54:4, 14; Jeremiah 1:8; 10:5; 17:8; 23:4; 30:10; 40:9; 42:11; 46:27, 28; 51:46; Lamentations 3:57; Ezekiel 2:6; 3:9; 34:28; Daniel 10:12, 19; Joel 2:21, 22; Micah 4:4; Zephaniah 3:15, 16; Haggai 2:5; Zechariah 8:13, 15; Matthew 1:20; 8:26; 10:26, 28, 31; 14:27; 17:7; 28:5, 10; Mark 4:40; 5:36; 6:50; Luke 1:13, 30, 74; 2:10; 5:10; 8:50; 12:4, 7, 32; John 6:20; 12:15; 14:27; Acts 18:9; 27:24; Romans 8:15; Hebrews 11:23, 27; 13:6; 1 Peter 3:6, 14; 1 John 4:18; Revelation 1:17; 2:10.

2. John 14:27; 2 Timothy 1:7.
3. Proverbs 28:1.
4. Psalm 34:4.
5. Matthew 26:56.
6. Mark 16:19; Luke 24:50–51; Acts 1:9; Acts 1:1–3.
7. Deuteronomy 31:6, 8; 2 Chronicles 20:15, 17; Psalm 23:4; Psalm 27:1; Psalm 56:4; Psalm 91:1–5; Psalm 118:6; Haggai

2:5; Romans 8:15.

8. 2 Timothy 1:7.

9. 1 Corinthians 10:13; 1 Peter 5:8–11.

10. Matthew 16:24–25.

11. Hebrews 12:1–13.

12. John 3:30.

13. 2 Corinthians 12:9–10.

8. Sometimes Being Smart Just Isn't Enough: God, Give Me Wisdom

1. Isaiah 46:9–10; Revelation 22:13; Jeremiah 1:5; Psalm 139:1–4.

2. Matthew 10:30.

3. James 1:5.

4. Proverbs 2:6; Proverbs 8:12.

5. John 1:1–18.

6. 1 Corinthians 1:30; Colossians 2:2–3.

7. 1 Kings 4:29–31; 1 Kings 10:23–24.

8. 1 Kings 3:10–12.

9. 2 Chronicles 16:9.

10. Psalm 33:18–19; Psalm 34:15; Proverbs 15:3.

11. 1 John 1:5; Psalm 27:1.

12. Job 28:28; Psalm 111:10; Proverbs 1:7; Proverbs 3:7; Proverbs 9:10; Proverbs 14:16; Proverbs 15:33.

13. Matthew 23:27.

14. John 7:15; Matthew 11:25; Luke 10:21; Acts 4:13.

15. Psalm 119:97–100.

16. 1 Corinthians 7:3–4; Ephesians 5:22–33.
17. 1 Corinthians 6:19–20.
18. Ephesians 6:18; 1 Thessalonians 5:16–18.
19. Matthew 7:13–14.
20. Matthew 22:36–39.

9. Will I Ever Be Happy Again? God, Bring Good Out of This Bad Situation

1. Matthew 10:29–31.
2. Malachi 3:2–4.
3. Romans 5:3–5.
4. 2 Corinthians 1:3–7.
5. Colossians 1:24.
6. Romans 8:28–29.
7. Philippians 3:10–11; 1 Peter 4:12–14.
8. 2 Corinthians 4:16–18.
9. Matthew 16:26; Mark 8:36.
10. Romans 2:4.

10. Why Am I Here, Anyway? God, Lead Me to My Destiny

1. Genesis 1:26–27; Psalm 8; 1 Peter 1:15–20.
2. Jeremiah 1:5; Psalm 139:16; Ephesians 1:4.
3. Matthew 10:30; Luke 12:7.
4. Psalm 139:13.
5. Ephesians 2:10; Romans 1:20.

6. Esther 4:14; Genesis 45:4–5; Genesis 50:18–20.
7. Luke 22:42.
8. Romans 12:2.
9. Psalm 127:1.
10. Proverbs 3:5–6.
11. Isaiah 42:16.
12. Isaiah 30:18.
13. Ephesians 5:18–20; Colossians 3:17; 1 Thessalonians 5:16–18.
14. Philippians 3:8–10.
15. Revelation 21:5.
16. Matthew 25:21.

BIBLIOGRAPHY

Bibles

Holy Bible: New Living Translation. Wheaton, IL: Tyndale Publications, 1998.

The Holy Bible: Revised Standard Edition. Catholic Edition. Camden, NJ: Thomas Nelson & Sons, 1966.

The Holy Bible: King James Version. Illustrated by Barry Moser. New York, NY: Viking Press, 1999.

The Holy Bible: New International Version. Grand Rapids, MI: Zondervan, 1978; revised, 1984.

The New American Bible. Washington, DC: Confraternity of Christian Doctrine, 1970.

The New King James Version Holy Bible. Nashville, TN: Nelson Bibles, 2006.

Other Works

Alcorn, Randy. *Money, Possessions and Eternity.* Wheaton, IL: Tyndale Publications, 1989; revised, 2003.

Allen, Charles L. *All Things Are Possible Through Prayer.* Grand Rapids, MI: Revell, 1958; revised, 2003.

Aquinas, Thomas. *Summa Theologica.* 5 vols. Westminster, MD: Christian Classics, 1981.

———. *Summa Contra Gentiles.* 5 vols. Notre Dame, IN: University of Notre Dame Press, 1997.

Augustine. *The City of God.* Translated by Marcus Dods. New York, NY: Modern Library, 2000.

———. *The Confessions.* Translated by Rex Warner. New York, NY: Signet Classic, 2001.

Bounds, E. M. *The Complete Works of E. M. Bounds on Prayer.* Grand Rapids, MI: Baker Books, 2004.

Chesterton, G. K. *The Everlasting Man.* San Francisco, CA: Ignatius Press, 1993.

———. *Orthodoxy.* San Francisco, CA: Ignatius Press, 1995.

De Caussade, Jean-Pierre. *The Joy of Full Surrender.* Brewster, MA: Paraclete Press, 1986.

De Sales, Francis. *Introduction to the Devout Life.* New York, NY: Vintage Books, 2002.

Dubay, Thomas. *Faith and Certitude.* San Francisco, CA: Ignatius Press, 1985.

Eastman, Dick. *The Hour That Changes the World: A Practical Plan for Personal Prayer.* Grand Rapids, MI: Chosen Books, 1978; revised, 2002.

———. *No Easy Road: Discover the Extraordinary Power of Personal Prayer.* Grand Rapids, MI: Chosen Books, 2003.

Groeschel, Benedict J. *Arise from Darkness: What to Do When Life Doesn't Make Sense.* San Francisco, CA: Ignatius Press, 1995.

John Paul II. *On the Christian Meaning of Human Suffering (Salvifici Doloris).* Washington, DC: United States Conference of Catholic Bishops, 1984; reprinted, 2002.

Kempis, Thomas. *The Imitation of Christ.* New York, NY: Vintage Books, 1998.

Lehodey, Dom Vitalis. *Holy Abandonment.* Rockford, IL: Tan Books and Publishers, 1934; reprinted, 2003.

Lewis, C. S. *Mere Christianity.* New York, NY: HarperCollins Publishers, 2001.

———. *Prayer: Letters to Malcolm.* New York, NY: HarperCollins Publishers, 1998.

———. *The Problem of Pain.* New York, NY: HarperCollins Publishers, 2001.

———. *The Screwtape Letters.* New York, NY: HarperCollins Publishers, 2001.

Meyer, Joyce. *Be Anxious for Nothing: The*

Art of Casting Your Cares and Resting in God. New York, NY: Warner Faith, 1998.

Moody, D. L. *The Joy of Answered Prayer.* New Kensington, PA: Whitaker House, 1997.

Murdock, Mike. *The Assignment: Powerful Secrets for Discovering Your Destiny.* Tulsa, OK: Albury Publishing, 1997.

Scanlan, Michael, T.O.R., with James Manney. *What Does God Want? A Practical Guide to Making Decisions.* Huntington, IN: Our Sunday Visitor, 1996.

Smedes, Lewis B. *Forgive and Forget: Healing the Hurts We Don't Deserve.* New York, NY: Pocket Books, 1984.

Warren, Rick. *The Purpose Driven Life: What on Earth Am I Here For?* Grand Rapids, MI: Zondervan, 2002.

ACKNOWLEDGMENTS

Writing a book — even a small one like this — is a major undertaking, not only for the author but for everyone who is close to him.

I'm not too proud to admit that this was *not* an easy book to write. Unlike other areas of theology, which are still relatively uncharted and lend themselves more readily to speculation, prayer has been at the very center of spiritual thinking for thousands of years. It is not an exaggeration to say that billions of words have been written about the subject. Some of the most brilliant thinkers the world has ever known — as well as some of the greatest saints and martyrs — have contributed to the theological discussion. So when I initially had the idea for this project, I was more than a little intimidated by it. I still am.

In fact, there is simply no way I could have completed this book without the support, guidance, and assistance of many special individuals. So let me express here and now a heartfelt prayer of gratitude to God for making the following people a part of my life:

My inner circle of trusted readers. These were the first people to read each of the manuscript chapters as they were written and to offer me their valuable insights: my father and mother, Sal and Laura DeStefano; my brothers, Vito, Carmine, and Salvatore; my sister, Elisa; my wife, Kimberly; my best friend, Jerry Horn, and his daughter, Jordan.

My wife, Kimberly, especially, has been extremely supportive throughout this entire process. Not only did she provide me with many fine editorial suggestions to improve the book, but she also did a great job of boosting my confidence during those difficult times when the project stalled or lagged for one reason or another. No one has worked harder to make this book a reality.

I don't think anyone has ever had a better team of dedicated colleagues and assistants than I: Jordan Horn, Tracy Corallo, Danielle Malina-Jones, Lisa Amass, and my brother Carmine have been there every step of the way to help me through some of the toughest problems imaginable. Jordan and

Carmine, in particular, have assisted me in ways I could never hope to reciprocate. It would be impossible to adequately thank them for all they do for me every day of my life. Thank you!

I am a man who has been blessed with incredible friends, some of whom even went so far as to let me use their beautiful homes when I was writing and revising this book. I owe a tremendous debt of gratitude to David and Mary Weyrich in Morro Bay, California; Tom and Wendy Howey in the Hamptons; Ralph and Carolyn Giorgio in Sarasota, Florida; and Margaret Mary Ott in Winneconne, Wisconsin. It's certainly wonderful to be a writer when you have such generous and giving friends in your life!

Even though my background is Catholic, I tried very hard to make this book as acceptable as possible to all Christians and, wherever I could, to people of all faiths. To this end, I was extremely fortunate to have the input of many scholars and friends, especially Dick Bott, Dr. Theresa Burke, Judge William P. Clark, Father Michael Colwell, Dr. Michael Crow, Dr. Dick Eastman, Dawn Eden, Monsignor Anthony Frontiero, Bonnie Horn, Monsignor James Lisante, Tom McCabe, Janet Morana, Jimmy and

Carol Owens, Charles Scribner III, Mary Worthington, Brian Young, Fr. John Leies, S.M., S.T.D. — who read the manuscript as Censor Librorum and secured an Imprimatur from Bishop John W. Yanta of Amarillo, Texas — and, finally, Cardinal Renato Martino, president of the Pontifical Council for Justice and Peace, at the Vatican.

High on my list of people to thank are my friends at Doubleday, especially its great publisher, Steve Rubin, Doubleday Religion's publisher, Bill Barry, and my editor, Trace Murphy — all true gentleman and consummate professionals. The whole Doubleday team, in fact, has been fabulous to work with. I don't think there could be a more competent and caring group of individuals in the field of publishing. Special thanks to Michael Palgon, Elisa Paik, Darya Porat, Rudy Faust, Kelli Daniel, Preeti Parasharami, Judy Jacoby, Jackie Everly, Alison Rich, Janelle Moburg, Louise Quayle, and John Fontana.

Peter Miller, president of PMA Literary and Film Management, Inc., continues to be my biggest cheerleader and promoter. An extraordinarily bold literary manager and deal-maker, Peter has become a great friend and trusted partner in my work. As long as the "Literary Lion" is in my corner,

I know someone will be knocking down doors, pushing through barriers, and overcoming all kinds of obstacles so that what I write will be published and read by as many people as possible.

Michelle Rapkin, my former editor at Doubleday and the person who initially bought the idea for this book, remains one of my dearest friends. Indeed, she has been my literary conscience ever since I started writing spiritual books. Every chapter of *Ten Prayers God Always Says Yes To,* in one way or another, bears the imprint of her kindness and wisdom. I am lucky to have her in my life.

Father Frank Pavone, M.E.V., founder of the Missionaries of the Gospel of Life and the priest about whom I spoke in Chapter 7, is probably the person most responsible for this book's existence. Working alongside Father Frank is like having Thomas Aquinas, G. K. Chesterton, and C. S. Lewis right down the hall! It is not an exaggeration to say that most of what is good in these pages derives from ideas I have gotten from watching and listening to Father Pavone over the past two decades.

Jerry Horn, my coworker and closest friend, provided me with the same kind of critically important help on this book as he did on the last one. Not only did he steer me in the right spiritual direction dozens of times, he also made it possible for me to concentrate on writing by handling all the thousands of different problems, details, and challenges that go along with having such a busy life. Without Jerry's loyal assistance, neither *A Travel Guide to Heaven* nor *Ten Prayers God Always Says Yes To* would ever have been written or published. Thank you, Jerry — and thanks for all you do for my entire family!

Finally, I want to express my heartfelt gratitude to all the people who prayed for me, personally, during the time I was writing this book, and who continue to pray for me and for the book's success. There is not a single, solitary doubt in my mind that God has heard those prayers and that he has extended his loving and helping hand to me countless times and in ways I could never fully repay or be worthy of.

Thank you all and God bless you!

ABOUT THE AUTHOR

Anthony DeStefano is the acclaimed author of *A Travel Guide to Heaven.* He lives in New York.